P9-ECT-546

TAMING YOUR TURBULENT PAST

A Self-Help Guide for Adult Children of Alcoholics

Gayle Rosellini
and
Mark Worden

Health Communications, Inc.
Pompano Beach, Florida

Gayle Rosellini
Mark Worden
Roseburg, Oregon

Publishers: Peter Vegso
              Gary Seidler
     Editor: Marie Stilkind
Art Director: Reta Kaufman
Typographer: Lauri Muir

ISBN 0-932194-50-8

Published by Health Communications, Inc.
                1721 Blount Road
            Pompano Beach, Florida 33069

A NOTE FROM THE AUTHORS:

This book is not filled with scientific facts and data about what it's like to grow up in an alcoholic home. We have taken facts and data into account, but current knowledge about the adult child experience is in its infancy.

We have learned most from listening to men and women who have been willing to share their experiences with us. We believe that a good example is worth far more than a page of statistics, but we make no claim that the examples we present are typical or infallaibly true of all people who grow up in unhappy homes.

The people we have used to illustrate aspects of the adult child experience are real people. In all cases we have not used their real names and have disguised identifying data in order to protect their privacy. In one or two cases, we have drawn a composite portrait to illustrate a certain point.

For ease of reading, we have written *Taming Your Turbulent Past* in the first-person. When we are speaking of our clinical work with clients, the pronouns "I" and "my" can either refer to either or both of us.

This book could not have been written without the support of some special people. We would like to thank Steve Worden, Lynne Rosellini, Al Martin, Bill Morrison and Lou Powers for their willingness to discuss, debate, criticize and encourage our ideas. And a very special thank you goes to Alta Crawford, who helped more than she can ever know.

Our friends at Health Communications also deserve our appreciation. Our publishers, Gary Seidler and Peter Vegso, have been supportive and, even more important, available to us. And lastly, we would like to thank Marie Stilkind, who edited the raw manuscript with sensitivity and style.

To readers who are struggling to cope with the after-effects of growing up with alcoholic or co-dependent parents, we would like to say this: This book isn't for your parents, but for *you*.

Your well-being, your health, your relationships, your day-to-day happiness. Your life. That's what is at stake here.

Adult children of alcoholics are, after all, adults.

And adults take responsibility for their own lives.

Isn't it about time you started living your life instead of sloshing around helplessly in the backwash of your parent's turbulence, expectantly waiting and hoping for someone to toss you that magic lifeline of happiness?

Aren't you tired of waiting?

Let's begin now. Let's take a look at how a new under-standing, a new perspective and a willingness to practice new behaviors can become your lifeline to a more satisfying life.

Epigraph

Man is a multiple amphibian who lives in about twenty different worlds at once. If anything is to be done to improve his enjoyment of life, to improve the way he can realize his desirable potentialities, to improve his health, to improve the quality of his relations with other people, to improve his morality, we have to attack on all fronts at once.

And the greatest, and what may be called the original sin of the human mind is sloth, its over-simplification. We want to think that there is only one cause for every given phenomenon, therefore, there is only one cure — there is not! This is the trouble: no phenomenon on the human level, which is a level of immense complexity, can ever have a single cause — we must always take at least a half dozen conspiring factors into consideration . . .

— Aldous Huxley, 1960

Contents

DEDICATION

This book is dedicated to

Tracy Lee Rosellini, Jr.

May He Always Know He Is Loved

1

The Pursuit of Happiness

The trouble is not that we are never happy — it is that our happiness is so episodical.

— *Ruth Benedict*

"I vividly remember a time in my childhood when I would lie in bed at night yearning silently for happiness. I knew happiness was my basic inalienable right." Carmen, a 32-year-old mother of two, smiled nervously, self-consciously as she sifted through her memories and keyed in on her happiness-hunger.

"I knew it absolutely because beginning in kindergarten I dressed up like a Pilgrim in November, and pretended to chop down cherry trees in February, and exploded fire-crackers in July, all of this in celebration of our brave Founding Fathers who gave their all to guarantee us 'life, liberty, and the pursuit of happiness.'

"I mean, my God, being unhappy was positively un-American. I not only had a right to be happy, but a duty as well. Wasn't this country founded on the very idea that personal happiness was the highest and loftiest goal we could seek in this life?

"Shouldn't that be my goal, too?

"But there I was, odd-kid out, unhappy and ashamed to admit it. It seemed everybody else in the world was happy and laughing and having a good time except for me, the forlorn little girl hiding her fear and pain and loneliness behind a shy smile."

Carmen was six years old and already felt like a failure . . . but not a total failure. Even at that young age, she could muster a sense of hope, a tiny, timid glimmering that maybe, just maybe, happiness would happen to her the same way it seemed to happen to others. Her memories continued to unfold. "I believed that as I grew-up and got out on my own, away from family turmoil, away from the demands of teachers and parents and siblings, that I would achieve an emotional pinnacle of permanent peace and happiness where my problems would melt away and my life would run smoothly, without conflict or fear."

Carmen possessed a deep yearning, a longing for a magical state of well-being which, once found, she would never lose.

She believed happiness was a concrete thing, something she could search for and find like a lost toy.

She also believed, as most children do, that the responsibility for her happiness and health and satisfaction rested outside herself. If she was angry, it was because someone made her that way. If she was lonely, it was because someone neglected her. If she felt alienated, it was because someone had hurt her, lied to her, disappointed her, and failed to meet her most basic needs to be nurtured and encouraged and loved. And who was responsible for making Carmen so miserable and unhappy and depressed?

"Well, of course. That's easy," Carmen says. "It was my parents." There's no bitterness in her voice, no tremulous quaver of thinly concealed sarcasm or hostility. Carmen has moved beyond the blame game, moved beyond the victim stance. And as she learned more about her happiness hunger, she also learned about the universal experience of childhood.

The Universal Experience

When you were a young child, the responsibility for your safety and health and well-being rested with your parents. You were totally dependent on them for your survival, both physical and emotional. You couldn't feed yourself, clothe yourself, keep yourself warm. Without the help of others, you would have died.

So you were totally dependent.

But not totally helpless.

You learned quickly how to behave in order to get other people to do what you couldn't do for yourself.

How did you do this? How did a small baby control other people? How did you get big people to meet your needs?

You cried.

When you were wet, when you were hungry, when you were frightened, when you were cold, you cried.

And then in response to your cries, a big person cleaned you and fed you and comforted you and kept you warm.

Maybe.

Sometimes.

Not always.

As you grew older, you learned to control your environment — and the big people in it — in ways other than crying.

You learned to smile and act cute when you wanted approval and attention. You learned to sulk when you felt upset and to act stubborn when you didn't get your own way. You discovered when tears worked and when they didn't, when anger was safe and when it was dangerous. You learned to express your feelings and to hide them, to be honest and to lie, to love and to hate, to accept and reject.

This learning process is normal and natural. It is the universal experience of childhood, and each of us carries inside the emotional memories of that childhood dependence.

If you grew up in a family conflicted by parental alcoholism and co-dependency, you are undoubtedly carrying with you emotional memories of powerlessness and pain, fear and rage, confusion and the desire to control your unpredictable parents.

These feelings are not odd or unique or mysterious. They are the normal reactions of a normal child in a dysfunctional family.

Unhappiness in reaction to discomfort, conflict and uncertainty is the universal experience of all humankind.

This is part of what Carmen experienced. It is what every child growing up in a turbulent home experiences. Why should you or I be different?

These unhappy emotional memories may be buried, half-forgotten, unconsciously repressed, or consciously suppressed through an agonizing act of self-will.

But they exist.

Countless adults continue to suffer emotional and physical problems in their day-to-day lives because they are re-enacting the unresolved conflicts of their earliest years in an alcoholic family.

The same difficulties we had as children in our families seem always to re-emerge to damage our adult relationships.

In effect, we re-create the personal hell of our childhood unhappiness.

The Inevitability of Unhappiness

Personal problems and unhappiness are inevitable because human beings are born with a nervous system that makes us sensitive to physical and emotional pain.

Emerson wrote: "He has seen but half the universe who never has been shown the House of Pain."

We inhabit the House of Pain — or perhaps more accurately, Pain is one of the rooms in our house. For some of us it is a small room, a closet or a crawlspace. For others it is the living-room, a space we enter daily.

We learn from pain. We learn not to stick our hands in the fire and we learn not to call a big guy with a bad temper a dirty name, at least not so as he can hear us.

In other words, the ability to feel pain is adaptive. It helps us survive in a world that can be dangerous and demanding and full of threats. It helps us adjust to the reality that fire burns and people retaliate.

But many adult children of alcoholics have become over-sensitized to the threat of pain — that is, because of our childhood memories we have a tendency to over-estimate the likelihood and intensity of a threat to our present well-being. We've been hurt in the past and we expect to be hurt again.

How do we avoid further hurt? By armoring ourselves, by taking elaborate precautions, by defensiveness. We not only guard against vulnerability, we protect and overprotect.

Our extreme sensitivity makes us anticipate pain. Our memories make us relive our past suffering over and over again until our natural capacity to anticipate and experience suffering becomes over-developed.

That Which We Fear . . .

Living under a ubiquitous cloud of doom, we may sense threats where none exist, a feeling Shakespeare aptly described:

"Or in the night, imagining some fear,
How easily is a bush supposed a bear."

We may also exaggerate the dangers that do confront us, magnifying small incidents all out of proportion, and in so doing, we create a real crisis where none existed before.

For example, Amy, a 37-year-old grocery checker, sought counseling because her second marriage was in trouble. She complained, "You can't ever trust a man. They'll always run out on you when you need them most."

When asked about her family of origin, Amy described a tumultuous childhood in a family preoccupied by her father's drinking and her mother's frantic efforts to hide his bottles. After years of broken promises, fights and financial hardship, Amy's parents separated.

"They tried to hide it from me," Amy said, her voice breaking. "One day my father packed his bags and said he had to go away on a business trip. He never returned. At first, I suffered the horrible fear that he'd been killed. Why else would he stay away? When I discovered he was still alive, I was overwhelmed with fury. I felt betrayed. He'd abandoned me, lied to me, hurt me. I'd never forgive him for that."

And her mother! "Nag and complain, that's all she ever did," said Amy. "No wonder my father left. I vowed I'd never act like my mother; I'd never chase away someone I loved."

But during her first marriage, Amy found herself reliving her childhood fears. If her husband was 30 minutes late coming home from work, she became anxious and jealous. Her black moods lasted for days. She questioned his every move, suspecting him of lying, and accusing him of not caring about her feelings. Naturally her own panic and moodiness had an impact on their relationship. The more she nagged, the more her husband withdrew, and the more she feared he would leave her.

And he did.

That was five years ago. Amy remarried, but once again she was swept along, out of control, besieged by worry and mired in childhood memories of abandonment by her alcoholic father.

In her anxiety Amy found herself looking and acting and sounding like the mother she held in contempt.

"I don't understand it," Amy said. "I'm educated. I'm intelligent. But I feel like a helpless victim."

Regardless of how smart we are or how much money we make, none of us is immune from the harmful effects of the unresolved conflicts of growing up in an alcoholic family. Amy's college education prepared her to make a living, but it did nothing to make her feel more confident or more loved. Even people who make their living helping other people cope with their family problems can find it difficult to cope with their own feelings.

Steve, a successful 45-year-old psychologist with a happy marriage and two teenage children, came to me for a refresher session in stress management. A vital, hard-working person, Steve is a man who has always impressed me with his stamina and his caring nature. I also consider him to be one hell of a good therapist.

We were all shocked when Steve ended up in the hospital emergency room with chest pains. Fortunately, his heart proved sound. The doctor diagnosed Steve's problem as esophageal spasms. The cause: Stress.

I asked Steve, "Has anything unusual happened lately?"

Somewhat embarrassed, Steve said, "I guess you could say that. I just moved my mother into the little house behind ours. She's getting older and needs to be close to us, but every time I'm around her for more than a few hours, I get these spasms."

"Is she drinking again?" I asked, knowing she had a history of alcoholism.

Steve shook his head. "She's been sober two years now. I'm very proud of her." At that point Steve swallowed hard and pressed his hand against his chest. "Hell, I thought we'd worked out all our problems when she quit drinking, but look at me. She still gets to me."

Does that sound familiar? Do your parents still get to you? Are you still emotionally trapped by family alcoholism?

Getting Free

Taming Your Turbulent Past is about getting free from the resentments and anxiety and painful emotional memories adult children continue to carry from childhood into adulthood.

To get free, you don't need the permission or help of your parents. This is something you can do on your own, without their knowledge or any change in their behavior or lifestyle. This book is not about confronting and changing your parents. It's about confronting and changing yourself.

After surveying the turbulence and wreckage caused by family alcoholism, I have come to a startling conclusion, one which is often hard for adult children to accept. A startling conclusion and a starting point:

No matter how horrid the behavior,
No matter how neglectful, spiteful or cruel the conduct,
Alcoholic and co-dependent parents
Did the best they knew how . . .
Under difficult circumstances.

Our parents did indeed make mistakes — at times dreadful mistakes. And one way or another, many parents continue to do so. But seldom have I found an alcoholic or co-dependent parent who purposely wanted to inflict the kind of pain that children in alcoholic homes endure. So, yes, your parents did hurt you, and what they did to you was wrong.

Yet, under all the resentment and anger and pain, one truth rings clear. *All parents want to love and be loved by their children. All children want to love and be loved by their parents.*

Your mother did the best she could.

Your father did the best he could.

They made mistakes.

So did you.

Are you willing to let the healing begin?

2

The Paradoxical Personality

It is human nature to think wisely and act foolishly.

— *Anatole France*

Each of us is a unique individual. This is something we take for granted. Yet, amazingly, underneath the uniqueness and individuality of each situation, there is a likeness, a commonality of attitude and world-view that is shared by adult children who are conflicted, angry, resentful and unhappy.

I say amazingly because adult children invariably believe the awful anxiety, fear and confusion haunting their lives is peculiar to them alone. They feel singular in their agony, fearful and ashamed of . . .

. . . of what?

It's hard to put into words, but the feeling is real. It's like a slow burning ember, a smoldering sensation of dread, an inkling or intuition of trouble. From time to time it fades away, then it flares again, a feeling of sick tension, an actual physical pressure somewhere between the belly and the throat telling you something bad is about to happen.

And you can't control it. It's just there.

Have you experienced this emotional and physical state? It's common among adult children.

Does that surprise you?

Most adult children are relieved to find they are not alone, that many, many other people have experienced and survived these feelings, and have gone on to lead healthy and happy lives.

There's a little chagrin, too. A touch of unexpected embarrassment. I mean, it's kind of shocking to discover you've been suffering in secret shame, hiding the fact that you practically feel like an alien from outer space, only to discover there are thousands — hundreds of thousands — of other men and woman who are going through very similar emotions.

Is nothing sacred?

Are we not unique in our misery? Isn't our own personal brand of suffering so extraordinary and unusual that it's almost beyond the reach of puny human understanding?

Perhaps.

And perhaps not.

Looking For Explanations

I've actually had people look at me in awe when I describe the feeling of dread — of badness — that is so common in adult children.

"How did you know?" Deanna whispered. "How could you know? I've never told anyone. Are you . . . are you psychic?"

Deanna was almost insulted when she discovered I possessed no supernatural powers, no special ectoplasmic connectedness with the Spiritual Force. You see, she felt her pain was so unique and incomprehensible that it was beyond the understanding of another ordinary person.

A person like me.

Because our feelings and behavior baffle us, we have a tendency to lean toward the exotic or the unorthodox to explain why we are the way we are.

"Mars is retrograde right now and that's very bad for a Virgo and a Capricorn," Carla explains. "That's why Tom and I are fighting so much lately."

"During the French Revolution, in one of my past incarnations, I was guillotined for stealing a loaf of bread," Leslie says, rubbing the back of her neck. "That's why I get these terrible pains."

"I'm not feeling well because my aura is muddy."

Statements like these indicate we are looking outside ourselves for explanations and solutions to our problems. This is called externalizing, and it is a common trait among people who are unhappy with their lot in life.

Internal Changes

We have no control over the planets or what happened 200 years ago or the color of our aura.

We can change nothing but ourselves.

This is important for us to keep in mind because in our search for explanations and solutions, we must focus our attention on those things over which we can exercise some power.

And we must be prepared to face some discomforting facts about the world and some unpleasant truths about ourselves. One of the most important things we can learn is that there are many things in the world that we can neither control nor change.

- We can't change the past.
- We can't control the behavior of our parents or other loved ones.
- We can't always get our own way.

All uncomfortable facts. But useful, fundamental to any serious efforts to change.

If you want to, you can keep butting your head up against the wall trying to control and change things over which you have no power, but you are going to end up being one miserable and frustrated individual. A sorehead — in more ways than one.

A Pattern of Paradox

Adult children seem to move from one crisis to the next, rarely pausing to notice the process going on underneath. Yet only by understanding the larger patterns in our behavior do the individual incidents and events begin to make sense.

A prominent pattern for many adult children is paradox.

A paradox is something which is seemingly absurd and self-contradictory, yet is in fact true. The term adult-child is a paradox, yet we understand its meaning without explanation.

Rhonda provides a good example of paradoxical behavior. For years she suffered from the paradox of love-hate. As a young girl, Rhonda had developed a close and loving relationship with her mother, a woman who seemed like a rock of stability in a homelife made stormy and chaotic by the father's drinking. "Mother and I shared many secrets and confidences," Rhonda recalls, "and together we protected the younger children from some of the worst aspects of Dad's alcoholism."

While Rhonda was away at college, her father entered treatment and sobered up. "It seemed like an answer to a dream. Finally, my mother and younger brothers could have some peace and happiness at home, a blessing I had never known."

Throughout the next few years, Rhonda developed a new and satisfying relationship with her father. Sober, he was witty, charming, responsible and caring.

But a new problem arose . . . her mother.

"I began to notice that during my visits home, my mother sulked and made cutting comments whenever I spent more than a few minutes conversing with Dad. Alone in the kitchen with her, I had to listen to a long list of complaints and if I refused to sympathize, she retreated into a hurt silence."

The visits home became a nightmare. Rhonda dreaded them, yet she felt compelled to return. It was her duty, she felt, to bring a little light and joy into the house for the sake of her younger brothers, if for no other reason. She also felt a need to help her mother, to make her stop being so negative and unhappy.

"I still love her dearly," Rhonda told me, "but she's driving me crazy. All she wants to do is talk about the past. She just can't accept that things are different now. I try to talk to her but she's so set in her ways, it's no use. I hate myself for feeling this way, but I can't help it. She makes me so mad!" Rhonda started to cry. "Sometimes," she sobbed, "I wish she'd just die and leave the rest of us in peace."

Rhonda's statements imply that her unhappiness and conflict are all her mother's fault. If only her mother would change, Rhonda thinks, everything would be all right. But the resentment and guilt and self-hate that Rhonda feels are not her mother's problem. They belong to Rhonda.

And if her mother dies?

No matter how much you'd like to believe that death or distance means you no longer have to deal with your feelings about your parents, you are wrong. The feelings you have for your parents — both good and bad feelings — remain alive in your mind and close to your heart.

Test Your Paradox Potential

Answer 'Yes' or 'No' to the following questions:

1. Do you feel an inner rage which you don't dare show to other people because it is too powerful to unleash?

2. Do you hide frequent fears behind a facade of bravado, wit or chronic pain?

3. Do you frequently feel like your spouse or parents are trying to control you when they can hardly run their own lives?

4. Do you long for warm and caring relationships, yet feel left out or overwhelmed by other people?

5. Do you suffer from feelings of low self-esteem because other people fail to appreciate all that you have to offer?

6. Do you resent your parents' alcoholism and co-dependency while suffering from compulsive behavior yourself, such as eating binges and fad dieting; reliance on marijuana, tranquilizers or alcohol, compulsive spending or gambling?

If you answered 'YES' to any of these questions, you can safely assume that you are plagued by paradoxes.

Paradox and Self-Esteem

The adult-child's life is filled with contradiction and ambivalence, by love-hate, pride-shame, greedy-giving. The experience of feeling these intense paradoxical emotions perpetuates your confusion and sense of alienation.

Pride prevents you from stepping back and making an honest and self-critical analysis of your own negative behavior.

You remain blind to the process going on underneath, to the larger pattern that clearly shows you are the perpetrator of your current unhappiness.

But can you really fool yourself?

The subtle knowledge that you are daily violating your higher values with your inexplicable feelings of hate and greed fill you with shame and self-contempt.

How can you like yourself? How can you have high self-esteem when deep inside your heart you are concealing so much anger, resentment and pettiness?

Now think about this for a moment. What I'm telling you may shock and offend you, but it's something you already know intuitively.

You know your inner self better than anyone else does.

Your feelings of low self-esteem are an accurate reflection of your inner reality. You don't like yourself because no matter what kind of bright and shiny face you show to the world, you know your heart is full of negativity, bitterness and anger.

No amount of success or money or recognition can make you feel good about yourself if your inner reality is a dark mass of justification, blame, denial and paradox.

Examining the complex nature of the adult-child's paradoxical personality is not an easy task. Nevertheless, that is one of the main purposes of this book. It seems vital and necessary, since self-critical analysis is an indispensable part in the process of self-change.

Without the knowledge that comes from fearlessly inspecting our most negative characteristics, we end up dooming ourselves to repeat in ignorance the patterns of the past that have brought us only hate, fear, loneliness and pain.

Isn't it time to give up our petty egos, to forget the fear of appearing vulnerable, weak and less than perfect? We are after all only human.

And happily, humans possess the wonderful capacity to make changes.

In fact, as Aldous Huxley put it:

"There's only one corner of the universe you can be sure of improving, and that's your own self."

3

Paradox 1: Anger and the Smiley Face

There's daggers in men's smiles.

— *Shakespeare*

During your childhood your parents did things that made you feel angry. They criticized you, punished you, ignored you. They embarrassed you, manipulated you, spanked you. They made you do things their way when you wanted to do it your way.

Each time this happened, you felt something unpleasant — anger, frustration, hurt. This is completely normal and natural, the universal experience of childhood we talked about earlier.

If your parents were knowledgeable and healthy and well-adjusted, they probably went out of their way to offset each of your negative experiences with a positive one.

If your parents were knowledgeable and healthy and well-adjusted, they probably encouraged you, rewarded you, approved of you. They protected you, trusted you, cuddled you. They gave you the opportunity to experiment and learn, and when you fell flat on your face, they picked you up and kissed your hurts and let you cry until you felt better.

In families where each member is nurtured and allowed to express his or her feelings openly and honestly, children have the opportunity to deal with their angry, hurt feelings before deep resentments develop and fester. They learn the art of give and take. They learn to think of anger as a temporary condition, something they can experience, then let go. They become free to experience more positive emotions — joy and love and laughter.

In the real world these nurturing, healthy families are as rare as 50 carat diamonds.

In the world of alcoholism and co-dependency they are non-existent.

The nature of the alcoholic family guarantees that you grew up with unresolved feelings of deep hurt.

Your parents, overwhelmed by their own problems, were unable to nurture you, cushion your falls or kiss away your tears. They may have tried, really tried to be good parents, yet resentments developed and grew. You remember the things your parents did that frightened you, made you feel vulnerable, abandoned or unloved. You remember the fights, the unreasonable demands, the emotional distance, the pain. At times you probably felt your very existence, both physical and emotional, was threatened. Perhaps you even wanted to die.

As a child you had no effective way of coping with your fear and anger and deeply-felt resentments. You were unable to speak up for yourself, you were powerless, a victim of your small size and your limited years.

When your parents knowingly or unknowingly did things that hurt you, you stashed your pain away and did your best to pretend that everything was all right. You put on your smiley face and hoped and hoped and hoped things would get better.

Maybe they did.

You moved away and started your own life. You got a good job or fell in love or started a family of your own. Perhaps your parents even recovered. From all outward appearances you are a success. You should feel happy — not continuously ecstatic or euphoric, but relatively satisfied.

So if life is going so well, why do you feel so bad?

Still Pretending After All These Years

I have been constantly impressed by how good adult children seem to be. Logic dictates that men and women who grew up in the frightening and abusive environment so common in alcoholic homes would turn out bad — criminals, deviants, sociopaths, jobless down-and-outers and no-goodniks.

On the contrary. Alcoholic homes seem to produce more super-achievers than bums. But scratch the shiny surface and the picture isn't so pretty.

• Shana was a cheerleader and home-coming queen in high school and she won a full tuition scholarship to college. Attractive and intelligent, she managed to combine marriage, children and a career. Her friends and family admired her and looked to her as a role model. She seemed to have everything in her life under control. Why did she have a nervous breakdown at age 29?

• Ted is 30, fun-loving, handsome and bright. His law practice is thriving and he's considered one of the most eligible bachelors in town. He says he wants to settle down and start a family. He certainly has no trouble getting dates. Why can't Ted maintain a relationship for more than a few months? Why is he so lonely?

• Alisha is generous to a fault. She's always the first one to volunteer to help in an emergency, she gives thoughtful gifts for no reason, and her smile is ever present. Why do her sweet compliments contain little hooked barbs? Why can't she keep friends?

• Francine pulled herself up by her own bootstraps, working her way through college, finding an excellent job and finally marrying the boss. Her car is new, her clothes gorgeous, her home a dream. Her husband adores her and her son is the best dressed kid in the first grade. She's achieved everything she ever hoped for. Why does she fall into periods of black despair? Why does she binge on junk food, then fast for days to take the weight off? Why does she drink too much?

Facing Your Inner Child

Are you like Shana, Ted, Alisha or Francine? Are you still hiding your anger and resentments behind a smiley-face, pretending nothing is wrong. It was a strategy that worked for you when you were a child, but if you continue this pattern as an adult, it will prevent you from enjoying the freedoms that adulthood brings. Hidden resentments have the power to control your life, making you miserable. And they don't go away on their own.

In order to lead a happy adult life, you must first make peace with your angry, frightened inner child. Until you begin to work through your stockpile of buried childhood resentments, you will be restricted in your ability to enjoy the pleasures of adulthood.

You can assume you are suffering from buried resentments and anger if . . .

— you are extra sensitive to criticism and personal slights and your feelings are easily hurt.

— injustices done you in the past occupy your mind to such an extent you can get in a black mood just by thinking about them.

— you poke fun or make cutting comments about those you love.

— you frequently feel a pressure or tightening in your throat and chest which makes it feel like it's hard for you to breathe.

— you suffer from frequent headaches, backaches, neck aches, stomach aches, jaw aches or other aches and pains which don't respond to standard medical care.

— you frequently feel left out, unappreciated, or taken for granted by the people you care about.

— you feel life is plain unfair.

— you have a weight problem or go on eating binges when you're upset.

— you are in a frequent state of irritation, primed to blow, and that scares you because you have a deep suspicion that way down inside you lurks a monster, an ax murderer, a fiend capable of God knows what kind of destruction. If you ever let go, God help the world.

Why Not Let A Sleeping Dog Lie?

"Listen," my friend Jaime said to me. "I have no desire to dwell on all that old pain. What's done is done, and there's nothing I can do to change the fact that my father, the great and wise doctor respected by the entire medical profession, was a mean drunk. I'll never forgive him, so it's a waste of time even talking about it."

"You talk about it a lot," I said.

"Just forget I brought it up," she replied. "Let sleeping dogs lie. Most of the time I never even think about it."

Unfortunately for Jaime, her resentment toward her father wasn't a sleeping dog. It was more like a clawed monster that refused to stay buried in the graveyard of her memory. Several doctors had told her that her recurring health problems were caused mainly by muscular and vascular tension brought on by chronic, unrecognized stress.

Unrecognized. It's a key word.

Most of the time our past resentments are in a state of limbo. Our conscious mind is oblivious to them. But if we believe we are totally free of resentments we are probably deluding ourselves. Every once in a while, our defenses break down, allowing the clawed monster to break free, ripping our serenity to shreds, starting the chain reaction of emotional and physiological stress which is so harmful to us.

You might have insomnia or frightening dreams. Or physical symptoms of stress such as frequent headaches and backaches or stomach problems. You might have an argument with your spouse or lover that inflames old buried hurts, causing you to respond with an intensity of feeling way out of proportion to the present provocation. In a new situation, old fears and resentments may arise making you feel panicky and vulnerable for what appears to be no reason at all.

But there is a reason.

While the particular childhood incident with your parents may be hidden in the back alleys of your brain, the remembered feeling is imprinted on your nervous system. When a present situation arouses buried childhood memories, you may not consciously recall the past incident, but you re-experience the emotional pain.

Stressful memories will be continually reactivated because people and situations in your current life will resemble people and situations from your past. This is no accident. We seek the familiar, the "normal". And no matter how dysfunctional your family of origin may have been, to you it represented the "norm".

Continuing the Same Old Patterns

In an effort to maintain continuity, we often blindly pick new people and new situations which resemble our past (bad) ones.

For example . . .

- One of your parents was alcoholic and you marry an alcoholic.
- One of your parents was dictatorial, the other passive; you and your mate follow the same pattern.
- You find yourself starting to act just like the parent you hold in contempt.
- You find yourself treating your children in the same hurtful manner your parents treated you.
- You find yourself "re-living" the same marriage, job, money or health problems that one or both of your parents went through.

- You find yourself treating your mate in the same hurtful way your parents treated each other.
- You find yourself trying to maintain the same rigid control of your life and family that you felt your parents unfairly demanded of you when you were young.

The Victim Stance: A Self-Made Obstacle To Freedom

Adult children often think of themselves as victims of misfortune, of cruel fate, an unfair world and their parents' mistakes. "Alas," wrote Emerson, "that one is born in blight, Victim of perpetual slight."

A victim is a person who is truly not at fault; he or she has not knowingly contributed to the cause of their problems. When you were a young child living in a turbulent home, you were a victim.

You're not a child any longer.

As an adult you no longer have to play the role of the child-victim. You can take responsibility for your life and health and happiness.

Yet, hidden resentments can make you feel victimized by the people you care about, compelling you to repeatedly act out the old negative patterns of your unhappy childhood.

The victim stance is a strange phenomenon. It's an almost invisible alignment of perspective and thought, invisible because it seems, well . . . so right.

You feel wronged. Something bad has been done to you and somebody bad is to blame. You have divided the world into right and wrong and you stand on the side of right. You are innocent of any wrong-doing. You are justified, therefore, in feeling angry. You have a right to get even, to hurt the people who have caused you pain. You believe that by hurting, blaming, condemning, excluding or shaming those who have done you wrong, you will feel better.

Such actions don't really work.

When you blame and hurt and condemn, it is you who bears the burden of hate and anguish and unforgiving vengeance. The weight of your own pain crushes you rather than the wrong-doer.

Remember Alisha of the sweet smile and barbed tongue? Her hidden resentments made her feel constantly under-valued and unappreciated. She felt like a victim. She tried so hard to make people happy, and still they hurt her.

"Why?" she agonized during our first meeting. "Why do people I trust betray me?"

Alisha tried to win affection with gifts and favors, and she couldn't understand why friends and lovers deserted her.

She didn't know that affection cannot be realized in an atmosphere of veiled accusation, sarcasm and guilt-inducing martyrdom.

Alisha had known for years that she carried a number of resentments towards her alcoholic father and co-dependent mother. Ever since she was a child, Alisha felt guilty and controlled and afraid of hurting her mother's feelings.

Her mother was such a wonderful person. So kind, so thoughtful, so caring. And with all she had to put up with, too. The woman was a saint.

Hating her father was something Alisha could understand and justify. After all, he was a drunk. But only a truly awful person, Alisha thought, could harbor the amount of anger and resentment she felt for her own mother.

Alisha rated her self-esteem at zero. "All I've ever really wanted," she said, "was for people to like me and admire me. I wanted to be loved. Fat chance!"

Following her mother's lead, Alisha became a gift-giver and favor-granter. She tried to be kind, thoughtful and caring. Just like Mom.

But each gift had a long string with a hook on the end of it with a message that said: *Love me. Realize my value. Pay attention to me. Don't criticize me. You owe me.*

If the recipient of Alisha's largesse failed to heed the unspoken message, Alisha felt justified in retaliating.

Just like Mom.

Alisha's mother had taught her to be a nice girl, and nice girls smile a lot, and they're passive, and they don't get angry and lose their temper. No, sir. Nice girls never openly criticize.

They cut with one well-aimed slash of the tongue.

They drown their victim with syrupy-sweet poison.

They play the hurt victim.

They use guilt to control and manipulate.

Nice girls can be the worst bitches.

Sometimes Alisha would feel depressed and sad for weeks at a time. "I was so lonely. I'd make friends with a new person and everything would be fine for a while, then pretty soon they'd start treating me rotten. I always let people take me for granted. It really hurt my feelings whenever that happened."

Today Alisha is a lot less sweet. She doesn't give as many gifts. Or hooked barbs. She's developed and maintained several interesting relationships with both men and women and she no longer goes around feeling unappreciated all the time. The changes came after she practiced the exercises that follow to help her acknowledge and overcome her backlog of pent-up resentments.

"I blamed everyone else for my unhappiness," Alisha now admits. "I felt betrayed and angry if people didn't treat me exactly how I wanted them to. I finally realized that I couldn't force people to like me by making them feel guilty if they didn't do what I wanted. All my gifts and favors were merely ways of trying to control the people around me. I never really gave of myself. All my giving was really a cover for my selfishness. Letting go of my resentments was hard because it made me accept the fact that I was responsible for my own unhappiness. But it gave me hope, too. Now I am happy, no strings attached." For the first time in her life, Alisha learned how to give without demanding an immediate reward for her generosity.

Alisha's situation illustrates an important principle:

As long as you maintain a victim stance, you will never find a lasting solution to your inner misery. As long as you cling to your hidden resentments, you will feel like a victim.

We must let go of our resentment and anger and pain, for the price we pay for not letting go is too high.

Let go.

Why do you cling to resentment? There is nothing you can do about the wrongs of your childhood. Why hold on to the past when it keeps you from hope and love and peace in the present?

Let go.

4

Now What?

None of the psychotherapists I knew raised the possibility of forgiveness with their patients. It was no wonder that people's hurts have to be studied, analyzed, emoted about, desensitized, pored over and rarely cured. For in the end there is no answer to profound hurt except: Yes, that must have hurt a great deal. Now what?

— *Arthur Egendorf*

"I wish it didn't hurt so much," Nadine choked out, the tears streaming down her face. "I can't stand feeling this way. I try not to think about it, but it won't go away. Sometimes I get so angry! Why me? Why did this happen to me? I want to kill myself sometimes — just put an end to my suffering — but I'm too chicken, too afraid of not doing the job right and hurting myself. God, I wish I could just disappear!"

What makes Nadine hurt so badly that she'd rather die than endure another day of suffering. A broken back? Cancer? Infected third degree burns?

No. Nothing so visible, nothing so tangible. Not an injury or disease to be cured with an antibiotic, chemotherapy, or a skin graft. A hospital's arsenal of potent pain-killers holds no power to relieve Nadine's agony.

Nadine suffers emotional pain, the spiritual anguish of anger, hate, bitterness and resentment. She wants to free herself from her pain, but doesn't know how.

Emotional pain hurts every bit as much as physical pain. And in this life none of us can escape the misfortunes and tragedies that bring emotional pain. We will all suffer. Those we love will disappoint us, desert us, die on us. We will be subjected to thoughtlessness, small acts of cruelty and devastating calamities.

Emotional pain cannot be avoided. It can only be dealt with. This is an enduring reality beyond our mortal ability to alter. We can only accept its inevitability. As Arthur Egendorf notes, after we acknowledge the hurt, the question remains: Now what?

Ordinarily, pain is a temporary part of life. But for a child growing up in an alcoholic home the pain can become constant.

How does the child survive in these conditions? How did you do it? For you did survive! You did make it to adulthood with at least a semblance of sanity. How does an inexperienced child manage this remarkable conquest over indescribable emotional anguish?

Some children have the help of an understanding adult — a grandparent or aunt, a teacher, a minister — a person who makes the child feel safe and valued, who models healthy ways of coping with the pains of life. With caring adult intervention, children in alcoholic homes needn't become emotional wrecks.

But how many children are fortunate enough to receive such help? Nadine certainly wasn't. Her mother's addiction to alcohol and pills made every single day of Nadine's childhood a roller-coaster ride of uncertainty and fear. Her father, a successful businessman, paid the bills and kept the house in repair and worked . . . and worked . . . and worked. He didn't abuse Nadine; he ignored her. When she tried to talk to him about her mother's addiction, he closed his ears. When she begged her father to help her, understand her, love her, he picked up his briefcase and went back to the office, leaving her home alone to cope with her mother's increasingly bizarre behavior. If Nadine cried, her father turned away in stony silence. But if Nadine had dinner on the table at six o'clock and if she had her mother in a clean dress and lipstick when Daddy came home, it was a different story. He smiled at his little girl, told her jokes, called her his sweet princess, gave her money.

So Nadine did what she had to do. She did what most children in alcoholic homes do. She played the role that made her difficult life a little easier to bear.

And she hid her pain.

She buried it. It's just as if she dug a hole in the ground and dumped her pain and fear and worry under layers of earth and stone and mud.

Out of sight, out of mind. Or so the saying goes.

Anger As A Protection Against Pain

When you suppress your emotional and psychological pain, it doesn't simply vanish underground and decompose like so much compost.

It grows.

And it undergoes a metamorphosis.

You see, showing your emotional pain to others, especially to those you care about, makes you feel vulnerable. It makes you open to disappointment and hurt and embarrassment. The shadow of past failures and rejections color your expectations with fear. So a natural defense mechanism takes over to protect you from experiencing your pain.

Your hurt changes to anger.

Anger and resentment arise as a protection against pain. When someone hurts you, you become angry in order to protect your inner being from the pain you've learned to hide. Anger becomes your shield.

Anger, itself, is not bad. It is a part of natural life; an emotion that comes and goes in every human being. But when you unconsciously use anger as an armor plate against suppressed emotional pain, it becomes a major problem.

You accumulate resentments. Deep resentments that control your life, hindering your ability to experience joy.

It's no longer a question of a natural emotion coming and going. Anger becomes your very being. You are not sometimes angry, you are always angry. It is as natural to you as breathing, and like breathing, you don't even notice it most of the time.

Suppression of emotional pain works as a childhood survival skill. Unable to deal with your anguish in any other way, you buried it in order to survive. Not on purpose but as a defense mechanism against problems you were unprepared to deal with. Occasionally the clawed monster of your hidden pain roared out of the grave you buried it in but overall you survived.
Which is good.

But isn't there more to life than mere survival? Survival means you go on day after day, doing the same things again and again. For what? If you are merely surviving, your life has no significance. You feel accidental, meaningless, unfulfilled. You remain dull, your vitality drained, your creativity blocked by your ever-present fear and defensiveness.
Is this what you want?

As a child, burying your pain was not a bad thing. It was a necessary survival mechanism.
No more.

Now that you are an adult, all that buried pain is like a weight anchoring your feet to the ground. You cannot be free until you dig into the deep hole of your suppressed anguish, until you open your pain to the healing light of acceptance and forgiveness. Because, you see, for adult children forgiveness is the major path to freedom and growth.

For too many of us, it has been the road not taken.

The Power of Forgiveness

Your pain is buried by anger — layers and layers of anger on pain. To heal your pain, you must first let go of your anger and resentments.

You must forgive.
Forgiveness is the only way out.
Forgiveness is the path to healing and freedom.
Forgiveness is freeing yourself from the past, so that you can face the future unencumbered by resentments and bitterness.

But forgiveness is not an easy notion to grasp. "How," we ask, "can forgiveness be the only way out?"

Arthur Egendorf, a Vietnam veteran who became a therapist specializing in work with other Vietnam vets, came to understand the power of forgiveness, but only after a struggle:

"Forgiveness?" he asked himself. *"How's that possible? Forgiveness didn't fit in with any psychology I had ever studied. It was a concept that was foreign to me and certainly not something I had ever imagined doing. I had always associated forgiveness either with weak people or with saints, but I was struck with the boldness of the possibility. Could it be that someone could simply say 'I forgive you,' and wrongs of the most hideous kind could cease to weigh upon either party? As a rational thinker I objected. How's that possible? What's to keep you from forgiving the wrong kinds of things?"*

Like many others, Egendorf discovered that forgiveness does not mean you have to like what happened to you. It doesn't mean the people who hurt you were right and you were wrong. You don't have to agree with the people who hurt you in order to forgive them. But you do have to let go of your anger. Anger is a bondage to the past, and when you forgive, you are choosing freedom over bondage.

Forgiveness is a gift of love to yourself.

The choice is yours.
Do you want to expend your energy in getting even?
Or do you want to be free?

Moving Toward Forgiveness

Truly *letting go* of your resentments is not just saying, "You're forgiven," then walking away. The complex web of emotions that traps us when we feel wronged is not easily untangled by logic and noble intentions.

Forgiveness is a process that can be broken down into three distinct steps:

Step 1: *Acknowledging* your resentment and pain
Step 2: *Desensitizing* yourself to the pain
Step 3: *Releasing* yourself from the pain

In the rest of Chapter Four and in Chapter Five, I will describe a number of exercises that other adult children have found helpful in moving toward forgiveness by letting go of their anger and resentments. These exercises are most effective if you follow steps one, two and three in order.

Some adult children feel a tremendous feeling of freedom after practicing just one or two of the exercises. Those with deep burdens of pain and strong defenses often must practice regularly over a span of many weeks before they can experience the relief of letting go.

Although these exercises deal with painful childhood resentments, their purpose is not for you to wallow in a pit of old despair. Their purpose is to heal old childhood wounds so you can be free to enjoy your adulthood.

You don't need the help or permission of your family to heal your resentment wounds. These exercises are for you.

A cautionary note: Under no circumstances should the resentments and painful emotions uncovered in these exercises be discussed with your parents at this time. In later chapters in this book, we'll talk about healthy ways to express your feelings.

Two Acknowledging Exercises

You cannot heal your pain unless you first acknowledge its existence. Many adult children find it extremely difficult to admit the true nature of their resentments toward their parents because to do so seems almost like a form of betrayal.

One of the hallmarks of alcoholic families is the conspiracy of silence. The first rule children learn is, "Don't talk about family problems to outsiders!" It's not uncommon for that rule to be generalized into, "Don't talk about problems."

So it may be hard for you to admit the details of your deep hurt, even to yourself. But the first step in recovery is to acknowledge that a problem exists. Take that step now.

Acknowledging Exercise 1: Your Resentment List

Set aside some private time when you won't be disturbed. Using paper and pencil, prepare a list of your resentments toward each of your parents. Be specific. Describe each painful incident in detail. A general statement like, "My mother is a bitch," isn't very helpful because it's not specific enough. After writing out each conflict that hurt you, write down how the incident made you feel at the time.

For example, part of one adult child's resentment list looked like this:

Resentments Against My Mother

I resent that you made me go into bars looking for Dad when I was only eight years old. I felt frightened and embarrassed.

I resent the way your moods were so unpredictable. One day you'd smother me with attention and the next day you'd be cold and sarcastic. I felt inadequate and confused.

I resent that you give me the silent treatment if I don't do exactly what you want me to do. I feel guilty and unloved.

I resent that when I was in grade school, you kept making me go to the little store on the corner with a note asking for more credit when you didn't have enough money for food. They knew Dad had spent all the money on beer and they made snide comments to me. I felt ashamed and guilty.

Resentments Against My Father

I resent that you came to parent's night at school and you were loud and drunk and told a dirty joke. I felt mortified with shame.

I resent that you slapped me around for no good reason. I felt unloved and vengeful.

I resent that you'd get drunk and call Mom a "slut" and a "whore" and a "pig". I felt hatred and fear.

I resent that since you got sober, you act like we should all fall to our knees and kiss your feet in gratitude. I feel bitter and hypocritical.

After filling up a page or two, you will reach a plateau of feeling. It's not necessary to record every last hurt and resentment, although you may still have a few major ones remaining. Stop and rest for a moment. Take a few deep breaths. Relax. Let any remaining deep hurts come to the surface and add them to your list. Don't be afraid to cry. You may find yourself re-experiencing your childhood pain right now. Don't be afraid. You are taking a very important step.

Read your list again, allowing yourself to experience whatever emotions that come up.

Now shift your body into a comfortable position. Take a few deep breaths, inhaling and exhaling slowly and deeply. Allow your body to relax as you focus your attention on your deep breathing. Feel your body becoming heavy with relaxation. Release the tension from your forehead and neck and shoulders and back. Feel the relaxation spread down through your stomach and hips and legs. Spend a few minutes allowing the tension to flow out of your body and away.

Now inhale and exhale deeply and repeat these words silently to yourself several times:

I have been hurt and I have a right to feel angry.

Admitting my anger to myself will not hurt me.

My pain and anger can be healed through acceptance and forgiveness.

I am ready to accept and forgive.

Now close your eyes and sit back comfortably. While focusing attention on your deep slow breathing, silently repeat these words: *I am ready to accept and forgive. I am ready to accept and forgive.*

After several minutes you will want to open your eyes. Sit quietly for a moment before you stretch and move around. You have taken the first important step in healing the deep hurts of growing up in an alcoholic home. And you are preparing yourself to experience the joys of a full adulthood. Congratulations.

Acknowledging Exercise 2: The Journal

This exercise calls for you to write about your childhood hurts in what is called a stream-of-consciousness style. Write whatever comes into your mind, ignoring grammar, spelling and logic.

Logic can sometimes prevent you from acknowledging your anger and pain. Some of our most deeply felt hurts are clearly irrational. And we know it. Because we recognize that our anguish is based on unreasonable premises, we only succeed in adding guilt to our stockpile of bad feelings.

For example, it bothered Peter that his German-born father spoke with a thick accent and wore funny-looking, old-fashioned clothes. "It's stupid," Peter chastised himself, "but I get furious with him for being so damn foreign. He embarrasses me in front of my friends. It's not his fault, but it drives me crazy."

Marie resented her mother for working when all of Marie's girlfriends had mothers who stayed home. "I felt so neglected," Marie explains. "After Dad left, she had to work to put food on the table. I know that, but I still feel like she cheated me out of an important part of my childhood."

Don held a grudge against both of his parents because they refused to help pay his college expenses unless he went to a lower cost State college rather than the expensive private university where his best friend was going. "Hey," Don says. "I wasn't even that good of a student, but I really wanted to go to the other school."

Peter, Marie, and Don all realize that their anger and resentments are illogical, unfounded, and irrational.

And they still feel wronged.

When it comes to our feelings, it doesn't matter what actually happened.

What matters is what we think happened.

In other words, if we think we've been wronged, we feel as if we've been wronged.

Even if the person who hurt you had totally noble motives, even if your facts are completely inaccurate, even if events were out of human control, even if you instigated the trouble yourself, you can end up harboring deep feelings of being wronged.

And these feelings, which are based on false thinking, are just as real, hurtful and damaging to you and your relationships as feelings based on truth.

The purpose of this exercise is to uncover long-buried, illogical resentments. Use paper and pencil or a typewriter, whichever you prefer. Write as though you were talking directly to your mother or father.

Remember, this isn't an assignment for English Comp. Let your writing flow, don't fret about neatness, reach inside for the deepest hurts, wounds, humiliations, insults and nightmares of your childhood. If you find yourself blocked, don't worry. It's perfectly okay to start your Journal one day, put it down for a while, then pick up where you left off.

An important note: The purpose of the journal is to uncover the deep layers of your hurt without holding anything back. You may end up writing 30 pages of intensely private and painful narrative. *Under no circumstances should you show your Journal to your parents.* This exercise is for *you*.

The following excerpt is from a journal written by Helen, a successful registered nurse. It powerfully illustrates the anger and suppressed love she feels toward her father.

Dear Dad,

Today is my birthday, January 12. You forgot it again, on purpose this time, I'm sure. On this cold day I have decided to begin a journey of forgiveness even though the depths of my anger toward you make even the smallest step in that direction seem impossible.

Exactly 15 years ago today you stood in the front yard and handed me a present as the sun peeped out from behind the grey clouds to shine on us, and we both laughed and said it was a good omen. I loved you so much that day. I had on the new dress I'd made and I'd fixed my hair the way you liked it best and I really believed you'd stay this time instead of getting in your car and driving away like you always did. Then you said, "A man's got to earn a living," and you got in your car and drove away. Just like always. You didn't even look back at me. You didn't care. Mom got drunk that day and ruined my birthday. But you weren't there to see it. You were never there. It was always that damn job of yours. "A salesman has to be on the road," you'd say. I think you got that job purposely because you couldn't deal with Mom's drinking anymore.

What about me? What made you think I could deal with her if you couldn't?

I wanted to believe you cared, really cared about me. When I looked at you, I saw a laughing man with wide, brown eyes and I thought I saw love in those eyes. I kept hoping you'd rescue me somehow, but you never did. I don't think you ever really cared what I was going through. I remember the time I asked you to come to the school awards banquet when I got my honor roll pin, and you said you didn't have the time. You didn't have the time to come to see any of my plays either. But two weeks later I saw you in the bleachers in the gym cheering like mad for the basketball team. I guess you cared about basketball more than you ever cared about me.

How do you think that made me feel? I wish somehow I could make you see that I needed a father more than the team needed a cheering section.

You had time for everyone but me, and now you have the nerve to call me up and whine that I don't have any time to spend with my poor old sick dad.

I hate that! The way you try to manipulate me to do what you want. You never bother to find out what I want and need from you. It's always what I'm supposed to do for you.

I think the reason I refuse to see you is because I want you to know what it's like to feel abandoned and unloved. I want you to suffer the way you made me suffer. I want you to feel the same aching loneliness of being ignored by your own family. No wonder you're lonely now. All you ever cared about is yourself and now no one gives a damn about you.

Except me.

Damn it! I don't want you to be sick. I don't want you to die. After all these terrible years of hating you, suddenly I realize you might die and nothing will ever be the same again. Even after all you've done, I still love you and I want you to love me, too. Sometimes I think you'd die just to hurt me, just to prove you still have the power to make me cry.

I don't trust you, Dad. I may never trust you. But I wonder if my desire to punish you isn't depriving me of something very special by keeping us apart. I wonder if hurting you is worth the hurt it causes me. I wonder if I can ever forgive you . . .

Writing in her journal was a gut-wrenching experience for Helen, yet with each page she felt a layer of the heavy burden of her resentment lift. After each writing session, she spent about ten minutes relaxing and breathing deeply. When she felt totally calm, she silently repeated the following words several times:

> *The past is a burden of pain.*
> *The present is a gift of forgiveness.*
> *I choose forgiveness.*

In these first few exercises Helen began moving toward forgiveness. With practice she would discover the wisdom in Catherine Marshall's words:

> *"I learned that true forgiveness includes total acceptance and out of acceptance, wounds are healed and happiness is possible again."*

5

Defusing the Past: That Was Then, This Is Now

My family sent a thin filament far into my psyche like the webbed roots of grass spreading under a sidewalk. Years after I thought they could affect me so deeply, the roots of their beliefs pushed upward and cracked my life apart.
— *Blanche McCrary Boyd*

In the last chapter we saw how Helen took the first halting steps on her journey to forgiveness. After recognizing her resentments and suppressed love for her father, Helen had to make a choice between perpetuating the distance and anger between her father and herself or letting go of her childhood pain and perhaps gain a reconciliation with her father.

She wanted to accept her father's invitation for a meeting, yet she was afraid to do so. "I get too upset," she said. "I can't relax around him. I keep expecting the old bitterness to flare up and I'm a nervous wreck by the time the evening's over."

Helen was so worried over what had already happened and what might happen, that she was unable to experience any joy in what was actually happening at the moment. She needed help in overcoming her memories of past pain and her expectations of future pain. After practicing the following two exercises for several weeks, Helen called her father and they set a dinner date. Much to Helen's surprise, the evening went smoothly. "Guess what?" she said. "I actually enjoyed myself."

Two Desensitizing Exercises

Acknowledging your buried resentments can stir up all sorts of old childhood memories. Painful memories. The feelings you experience as you sort out your suppressed hurts can be so troubling that your most immediate and spontaneous emotional response is to push them back down again. Down, away, gone, out of sight, buried . . .

. . . but not forgotten.

The next two exercises can help you get past the pain of your emotional memories by bringing them into the healing light of forgiveness.

Desensitizing Exercise 1:
Relax and Imagine

First, read through the instructions for this exercise several times before you try it.

Decide which resentments to work with on this occasion. You may want to read through your Resentment List and Journal.

Select a quiet room where you can have around 30 minutes of uninterrupted privacy. Sit in a comfortable chair and adjust yourself so that you are as relaxed as possible.

Close your eyes.

Now, consciously relax all your muscles, beginning with your feet. Feel the relaxation move slowly up through your legs, your hips and stomach, your chest, your shoulders and arms, your neck, your face and jaws, your forehead and eyes and scalp. Relax your entire body. Take your time and relax.

Breathe through your nose, and draw the breath into your belly, which will be rising and falling with each breath. Become aware of your breathing. Breathe normally and naturally, a slow and steady pace.

Now, as you breathe out, silently and slowly say the word "CALM". Inhale slowly and with full awareness. Now, exhale, let your breath out slowly and again repeat the word "CALM".

Keep the muscles of your body relaxed and continue breathing rhythmically and easily, repeating the word "CALM" with every exhalation.

Continue for around five minutes.

Stray thoughts may pop into your head as you relax. Don't worry about them. Let them drift through your mind and gently discard them. Just keep repeating the word "CALM", breathing easily and rhythmically, and keeping your muscles relaxed.

Now as you're feeling very relaxed, mentally picture yourself and your parent together in a familiar setting. It may be your childhood home, or a family outing, or in a car. However it seems to you is perfectly fine, but force yourself to create this mental picture of you and your parent together.

Now mentally tell your parent about your inner feelings and your resentment and pain. Deal with whatever resentment comes to mind. Say all the things you always wanted to say to your parent, but couldn't.

Regardless of how your real parent would react, picture your imagined parent as listening to you attentively, nodding, and saying, "I understand."

Release your anger and pain and humiliation. Feel free to rid yourself of all negative and violent feelings, *remembering this is only a visualization exercise and not real life.*

If you start to feel frightened or tense, take a deep breath and exhale, again repeating the word "CALM" until your body again feels relaxed.

After around ten minutes of visualizing your parent listening as you release your anger, take a deep breath and pull your mind back to the present. Inhale and exhale slowly.

Now, do a body check. Does any part feel tense or tied in knots. Your jaw? Your neck? Your shoulders? Your stomach?

Become aware of your body feelings, consciously relaxing any muscle that feels tense. Let a warm feeling of relaxation flow through your body. Take as long as you need to feel calm.

Now again form a mental picture of you and your parent together in a warm and lovely meadow. Everything is fresh and clean and warm. You feel very safe, very confident. You and your parent stand facing each other, both of you relaxed and emotionally calm. As you smile at each other, the clouds overhead part and a golden ray of sunlight sweeps over the two of you, warming and healing and cleansing.

Neither of you speak, instead you bask in the warmth and freshness of the moment.

Bask in the healing sunlight for several minutes, enjoying each moment as you experience it. You feel very safe, very confident as you and your parent silently share this moment.

After five or ten minutes you will want to gradually open your eyes. Sit quietly for a while before you resume normal activities.

Remember, this is an exercise of mental imagery and not real life. Be careful not to act out your negative or violent feelings with your real life loved ones. Our purpose is to heal old hurts, not create new ones.

Desensitizing Exercise 2: Advantages and Disadvantages

The three previous exercises were designed to help you deal with your resentments on a feeling level.

This exercise asks you to use a rational and cognitive approach in dealing with your anger.

Step 1: Use a double column to list the advantages and disadvantages of clinging to your anger and acting in a retaliatory manner toward your parents.

Consider both the short- and long-term consequences of feeling angry. This is what Perry's list
for his father looked like:

Advantages of my Resentments	Disadvantages of my Resentments
1. It feels good to have someone to blame for my problems.	1. Blaming someone else keeps me from helping myself.
2. I have the right to be angry after what he did to me.	2. My angry thoughts and feelings often make me feel guilty and down about myself.
3. If I'm cold to him, he'll feel guilty and try to make it up to me.	3. He'll probably just be cold back because he doesn't like to be rejected.
4. He'll know I disapprove of him and maybe he'll change.	4. My disapproval hasn't ever made him change before. What makes me think it will now?
5. My resentments protect me from being hurt again. They keep me from giving him another chance to disappoint me.	5. They also prevent me from having any kind of decent relationship with him. I'm sad that there's so much distance between us.
6. My anger makes him feel bad and I want him to suffer for what he did to me.	6. When I spend my time trying to hurt him, I can't concentrate on the positive things in my life.

Step 2: Now review your list and ask yourself these
questions:
   a. Which is greater, the costs of your resentments or
   the benefits?
   b. Is it really in your own best self-interest to cling to
   your resentments?
   c. Does clinging to your resentments positively
   enhance your life in any way?
   d. Are your resentments useful? Do they help you
   achieve a desired goal or do they simply defeat you?

Since most of us want what is ultimately best for us,
honestly answering these questions can put you in the

proper frame of mind for the final stage of forgiveness — letting go.

Here's how it works.

Three Releasing Exercises

Forgiveness is releasing yourself from the past and facing the future with a renewed sense of freedom. Put more bluntly, forgiveness is freedom.

The words "I forgive you" have the power to lift the heavy burden of pain from your shoulders, the power to end years of bitterness and recriminations.

But if it is so simple, why do we resist it? Why is it easier for us to hate than it is to forgive?

Why?

Because we humans are strange creatures. We'd rather be resentful and right than forgiving and free.

Anger is a moral emotion. You don't want to let go of your resentments because you are consumed with a desire for justice.

What if the person you forgive goes out and does something wrong all over again?

What if you forgive something truly horrible?

Aren't guilt and blame one of the few ways you have of restraining the wrong-doer?

Don't wrong-doers deserve to be punished?

To ask these questions is proof that the meaning of forgiveness is not understood.

Forgiveness is not granted as a response to a promise that bad will never happen to you again.

Forgiveness simply means you accept the other person as he is, and you love him the way he is. Forgiveness means that you do not judge him. Forgiveness means you are again able to see the other person as worthy. It means you accept the person even when you do not accept the behavior.

Forgiveness means you no longer hold yourself in bondage to the pain you knew as a child.

Forgiveness is a gift to yourself.
It is a gift of healing.

Releasing Exercise 1:
What if . . .

This is an exercise of visual imagery. Its purpose is to reduce your resistance to the idea of forgiving the people who have hurt you. Read the instructions all the way through several times before you try it.

Decide in advance which parent you want to work with on this occasion. For our example, we'll use your mother.

You'll need around 15 minutes of uninterrupted privacy. Select a comfortable chair and relax your body and mind as you learned to do in the Relax and Imagine exercise.

When you are completely relaxed, close your eyes and silently ask yourself questions like these:
- What if I forgive my mother for humiliating me by being drunk at the reception after the senior play?
- What if I forgive my mother for not meeting my needs and understanding me better when I was growing up?
- What if I forgive my mother for making mistakes?
- What if I no longer blame her for being an alcoholic?
- What if I forgive her?

Now, create a mental picture of you and your mother. Imagine a conversation where you look at her and say:
I forgive you.
You are my mother and I forgive you.
Now, imagine your mother accepting your forgiveness. Experience each emotion as it surfaces. Allow yourself to feel each sensation forgiveness brings.

Now, picture you and your mother in the golden sunlight of a green meadow. Bask in the healing light for a few

minutes before you gradually open your eyes. Sit quietly for
a few moments and relax.

Releasing Exercise 2:
Re-Creating History

Sometimes it is easier to forgive our parents for the way
they behaved toward us if we develop an understanding of
their historical background. After all, our parents didn't
spring fully formed into adulthood any more than we did.
Your parents possess their own history of painful
childhood memories.

Angela's Resentment List and Journal showed that she felt
'controlled,' 'manipulated' and 'pressured' by her mother.

"I always felt like she was trying to live her life through
me," Angela claimed. "Why didn't she live her own life, for
God's sake, instead of always pushing me to do the things
she never did? She acted like I'd break her heart if I didn't
finish college and land some sort of fantastic job so she could
be proud of my accomplishments. She was content to be a
housewife, but she pushed and pushed and pushed at me to
find a career until I wanted to scream."

As part of releasing her resentments, I asked Angela to
research her mother's family background to see if she could
better understand her mother's motivation.

During a long conversation with her Uncle Sid, a mathe-
matics professor, Angela discovered that in her mother's
family, females were considered second-class citizens whose
sole function was to meet the needs of the menfolk. Angela
learned that her grandfather had taken her mother out of
school when she was sixteen and put her to work in the
family business.

"It was a shame, really," Uncle Sid told her. "Your mother
was a brilliant student, much better than I ever was, but in
those days it was considered a waste of money to send a girl
to college. She had such drive, too. After she married your
father, she put all that energy into her family but I know she
was terribly frustrated. She was born 40 years ahead of her
time. Today a woman with her intelligence would be

running a major corporation instead of one small household. I think what she wants, Angie, is for you to have the opportunities that were denied her. She wants you to have the chance to be your own person, not just an extension of the men in your life."

Understanding the old family value system helped Angela recognize that her mother's personal ambitions had been thwarted by societal forces beyond her control, and not by laziness and lack of interest as Angela had frequently accused.

This insight made Angela see her mother's 'pushiness' in a new light.

Where Angela had always taken her freedoms and opportunities as normal and natural, she could now appreciate that it was only through her mother's courage and determination that Angela had been treated as an equal to the male members of the family.

"I had to ask myself," Angela told me, "whether my mother's expectations for my success were more burdensome than my father's and grandfather's total lack of expectations for me."

To still better understand her mother's psychology, Angela went to the public library and pored over stacks of old magazines from the 1950s. This helped Angela understand why her mother had covered up for her father's drinking for so many years. In the fifties, Angela learned, treatment for alcoholism was almost non-existent. In those days a woman's job was to take care of her husband, comfort him, be submissive to his will.

After leafing through half a dozen old issues of magazines like *The Ladies Home Journal,* Angela began to comprehend that her mother had enjoyed none of the freedoms women today take for granted.

No equal pay for equal work.

No equal opportunity employment.

No credit apart from her husband's.

No reliable birth control.

Few rights as a thinking, feeling, competent member of society, apart from the rights conferred on her for being Mrs. Somebody.

And how many viable options did a woman in those days have if Mr. Somebody turned out to be an alcoholic?

Slowly, Angela's resentment began to fade. Her mother, she realized, had suffered, too.

Releasing Exercise 3:
The Most Difficult Person To Forgive

Relax your body and close your eyes. Picture yourself standing in the center of your childhood home. Now, say: "I forgive you" to everyone and everything that hurt you as a child.

Picture yourself as a young adult attempting to assert your independence from your family and say: "I forgive you" to all those who tried to hold you back and put barriers in your path.

Now picture yourself as you are now and say: "I forgive you" to every single person who is dragging you down or pushing you away.

Now let your mind wander over an instant replay of your life. See yourself as a child hungering for attention, craving a sense of importance and power. See yourself cringe in self-contempt at the memory of your teenage selfishness and moral failures. Picture yourself as an adult, impatient, critical, and self-righteous.

With your body relaxed and your eyes closed, talk to yourself now. Forgive yourself for being powerless and foolish and frightened. Grant yourself forgiveness for not being able to change your parents' alcoholism and co-dependence. Forgive yourself for your anger, for your pain, for the deep blackness hidden inside your heart. Accept yourself for the person you are, a new person born this day in forgiveness and freedom and light.

You are forgiven. Accept your freedom now.

6

Getting Beyond Denial

We so often respond inappropriately to a situation or to a person because the defense mechanisms of denial, repression, substitution or projection are operating to skew our own reactions and to cause us to misjudge others. Unhappily we do not expand into adulthood; we narrow into it. We do not increase and refine our range of responses; we limit them. Our defenses form a carapace around us, as the shell encases the crab, and we end by becoming as constricted as the crab.

— Joy Coudert
Confessions of a Failure

Denial is a prime trait of alcoholic families. Without denial, alcoholism and all the problems it creates could not exist except as rare curiosities listed in thick books on abnormal psychology.

Denial is a protective mechanism that allows us to avoid looking at realities that seem too painful for us to handle. It allows us to defend against a whole barrage of unpleasant thoughts, feelings and perceptions.

Thoughts such as . . .
> *My father — my strong and wonderful father —*
> *is a mean drunk and I wish he was dead.*

Feelings like . . .
> *My mother — my perfect and loving mother —*
> *is selfish and crazy and I hate her.*

Perceptions that . . .
> *Other people have great families and*
> *my family life is unspeakably horrid.*

And perhaps worst of all is the idea that . . .
> *All of these bad things happen because I am*
> *a flawed and terrible person.*

Denial allows us to cope with fear and disappointment and loneliness. It allows us to survive in situations in which we are powerless and impotent. It allows us to keep on loving people who behave hatefully, to stay in destructive relationships, to work harder and longer, to smoke too much, to drink too much, to eat too much, to blot out anxiety and stress with marijuana and tranquilizers, to medicate fatigue and depression with cocaine and amphetamines, and to obliterate loneliness with brief, meaningless sexual encounters.

If you grew up in an alcoholic family, you can safely assume that the habit of denial is a basic aspect of your personality.

Wait! Before you indignantly shunt this idea aside, stop and think about what you've already learned. Isn't the paradox of anger and a smiley face a form of denial?

Didn't you grow up in a family where negating your real feelings of frustration, fear, isolation, aloneness, stress or anger was a daily imperative?

Language of Denial

Listen carefully to yourself. Are you speaking the language of denial without even knowing it? Do any of these phrases ring a bell in your head?

— If I can just get through the next month (six months, year, five years), I'll be okay.
— I'll never end up like my mother (or father).
— I don't have negative feelings.
— I can't start taking care of myself until I start feeling better.
— All I need to do is lose ten pounds.
— I know it didn't work before, but this time is different.
— All I need is a little time to myself.
— I thrive on this kind of pressure.
— Don't worry. I'm fine!
— There's nothing really wrong with me, except I can't seem to shake this virus.
— I didn't do anything wrong.

If your language and thoughts are peppered with these kinds of statements, you have surrounded yourself with a wall of denial. And if you consistently deny feelings of anger, fear, frustration, stress, worry or inadequacy, you can be sure that the physical and emotional strain is taking its toll on your vitality and creativity.

Of course, it's perfectly normal for a person to want to deny the existence of a situation that causes discomfort, pain or unpleasantness. Denial has its uses, no question about it. As 19th-century humorist Josh Billings observed, "It is not only the most difficult thing to know oneself, but the most inconvenient one, too."

Who among us really enjoys grappling with the worst parts of our lives? It's perfectly normal for us to valiantly protect our ragged and tender egos from the ugly truths that leave us feeling vulnerable, weak and out of control. We don't want to hurt!

Many of us grew up in homes where it was not all right to make mistakes. If you were clumsy or foolish or silly, if you were caught in a lie or a mistake or a prank, if you embarrassed your parents or failed a test or asked the wrong questions, the reaction was . . .

"What's wrong with you? Are you stupid?"

"Can't you do anything right?"

"Get out of my sight!"

"Shut that smart mouth!"

"I'm going to really give you something to cry about (whack)!"

These kinds of messages set up an Either/Or thinking pattern. Either your behavior is perfect/Or it is rotten. Either you are good/Or you are bad. Either you are the best/Or you are nothing. There is no middle ground, no room for mistakes or failure.

Denial flourishes in this Either/Or atmosphere. How can you admit your weaknesses, your fears, your blunders, when doing so means bringing an avalanche of criticism, anger and rejection down around your head?

To avoid the unpredictable wrath of parents, the child in an alcoholic home becomes a co-conspirator in a fully orchestrated fantasy of lies, diversions, cover-ups and repressions. To a child who has no other experience, this seems normal.

For as a child you had no other wish than to be happy, to make your parents love you and take care of you, to make them act right and stop fighting so much. So you learned the art and science of denial well. You did it to please the most important people in your life — your parents.

Deirdre Adams grew up in a respectable middle-class family in which her mother frequently got her way by intimidating her husband and children with her fierce temper and insults. Mrs. Adams led a bizarre double life: Publicly she was the epitome of success, but privately she was a frightened and unpredictably violent alcoholic.

Deirdre recalled, "Living with my mother was like being trapped in some crazy episode of the Twilight Zone. She never drank during the day, only at night. Here she was, this brilliant real estate broker, chairman of the Mayor's task force, president of the hospital auxiliary, president of the PTA, the volunteer of the year, the whole works. Other people used to tell me how lucky I was to have such a neat mother. I didn't know who was crazy, them or me!"

At night behind the closed doors and drawn curtains of the family home, Mrs. Adams dropped her public persona. With each martini she became a little nastier. At any moment she might explode.

"More than anything," Deirdre said, "I dreaded the vicious insults and accusations my mother hurled at me when she got drunk and lost her temper. 'You don't care about anyone but yourself,' she'd say. She accused me of lying, of cheating and stealing. And later . . . well, there were boys . . . and the usual accusations."

Deirdre did everything she could to avoid incurring the older woman's fury. She hid when her mother was drinking. She became a stoic Little Stone Face around her mother because she never knew how her mother would react to a smile or a frown.

Deirdre found that the best way to keep her mother in line was by being a Perfect Daughter. Deirdre learned that Perfect Daughters are nice, they don't make mistakes, ask uncomfortable questions or have unpleasant emotions. Deirdre played the role eagerly.

As Deirdre grew to adulthood she presented an image of strength, success and accomplishment to the world. Yet by the time she was 30 years old, she found herself chronically dissatisfied, physically depleted and emotionally isolated. She had a vague sense that "something was off" in her life, but she didn't know what it was. Like most successful women she was an ardent believer in the benefits of self-improvement, yet the protective wall of denial she had built around the unpleasant realities of her life meant that her ability to grow and improve was seriously impaired.

As Deirdre described it, "I kept thinking one more class, one more group, one more book would give me the key I needed to start feeling good about myself and liking my life. I kept looking outside myself for an answer to my problems. I became an expert in stress management, dieting, aerobic conditioning, communication skills, consciousness expansion and spiritual openness. Every time I thought I was on the threshold of total awareness, I'd either get physically sick or have some disaster that needed all my time and attention to resolve. There was always something in my way."

The something was denial.

Does Denial Protect Us?

Many adult children, like Deirdre, come to believe that admitting mistakes or weakness or fear will bring automatic annihilation — rejection, blame, anger, ridicule, criticism or abandonment. You feel you must protect yourself at any cost. And though you want to have a happier life, the painful emotional memories of what happened when you were less than perfect as a child now prevent you from engaging in the searingly honest self-examination which is a prerequisite to all significant personal change.

You want to become emotionally free, but you find instead that you are trapped in the old roles and conflicts from childhood. Despite your intentions to "do it right this time", nothing changes.

Denial is our way of heading off the anxiety, fear and dread that are the legacy of our buried and painful childhood memories. We don't want to re-experience those terrible feelings.

Yet we are faced with a simple truth. It is impossible to confront and resolve the continued pain in our turbulent lives without making old wounds bleed a little, without re-experiencing some of the anguish we seek to escape.

For adult children one of the standard cliches of the 1980s rings hauntingly true: No pain, no gain.

The question facing us now is this: Do we go for the gain, or hide from the pain?

Do we dive behind our wall of denial, do we play it safe, do we continue in our constricted and fearful existence or do we summon the courage to fearlessly examine our lives and ourselves? Do we hide behind lies or do we leap beyond denial to face the realities of our lives with honesty?

What Is the Cost of Denial?

Denial has a purpose: It maintains the status quo by redefining reality.

It also has a cost: It allows destructive individual behavior to continue unabated. It permits dysfunctional family systems to thrive from one generation to the next.

When you find yourself redefining reality in order to avoid facing unpleasant truths, your sense of self is subtly eroded. You soon begin to experience a distortion of your higher values and an estrangement from your authentic self.

Who are you really? The perfect strong person you pretend to be, or the frightened and confused person who lies crouched behind a wall of denial? Do you really know anymore?

In time as denial increases, you may sense a feeling of being alienated from your family, your work, your friends and your mate. You are alone. Somewhere there is a missed connection and you don't know how to hook yourself back up to life. You feel you are not living a real life, you are playing a role, and you wonder how long the show can go on.

When we are caught in the grips of denial — and God knows it happens to all of us — we are telling ourselves and the world, "There's nothing wrong with me. I'm all right. I don't want to change because I don't need to change. I'm stronger than other people, more resilient, more resistant, more capable. Now get off my back and leave me alone."

In essence we are denying the negative and weak and dark side of our human nature. And let there be no mistake, each of us does indeed possess such qualities. Who among us is a faultless creature of innocence and perfection and strength?

Denial keeps us imprisoned. Awareness and acceptance break the shackles of the past. If we refuse to acknowledge and confront our habit of denial we are dooming ourselves to a restricted and barricaded existence.

Refusal to accept our negative, dark side allows that side to run us. By accepting as real all of our human qualities — both the light and the dark sides of our nature — we are better able to admit our human frailties. We free ourselves to conquer our weaknesses and forgive ourselves for our failings. We free ourselves to be fully alive.

Constricted by Denial

Denial blocks, obstructs or diverts the flow of communication. In denial we adopt a closed stance, as if we mentally cross our arms as barriers to protect and defend against unpleasant facts and feelings.

And denial takes its toll. We become emotionally crippled. The flow of ideas, thoughts and feelings are sifted through a distorting emotional filter which enables us to maintain our self-destructive behavior. We hear only what we want to hear, see what we want to see, say only what we want others to believe.

As Joy Coudert put it, ". . . we end by becoming as constricted as a crab."

Inevitably, we turn into liars and frauds, not only with other people, but with ourselves. Unfortunately we seldom recognize these traits in ourselves. If we did, we would no longer be in denial.

Everybody, not just adult children, practices a little denial now and then. It's pure human nature. The size 16 lady squished into the size 12 pants doesn't know what she looks like because her denial prevents her from standing before a full-length mirror. And the guy with the long strings of hair pasted from his left ear to his right thinks he can hide his bald head when it's right there in plain view. Relatively harmless denial. We all fall victim.

But adult children are trained experts in far more dangerous and destructive forms of denial . . .

— Adult children smoke at a high rate, even after they have developed lung and other diseases.

— An estimated 50% to 70% of adult children will develop chemical dependency problems of their own (compared to 10% to 15% of the general population).

— Adult children also have especially high rates of severe depression, suicidal thoughts, eating disorders, sexual dissatisfaction, stress illnesses and job burnout.

Any one of these problems can cause enormous unhappiness in a person's life. Many adult children suffer from two or three or four of these disorders in combination. One problem feeds off another, increasing misery exponentially until running away or disappearing or ending it all seem like the only way out.

Have you been to that dark place? Have you ever felt so lost and frightened and alone that you didn't think you could go on? Have you lain on your bed and felt the world close in on you . . . have you looked at your life and said it'll never, never, never be better.

If you have struggled with these agonizing feelings, please believe me when I say your life can be better and will be better if you can summon the courage to move beyond the constraints and constrictions of denial.

Opening Up

Think back to the atmosphere in your alcoholic family. What were discussions like? Were your parents open and receptive to questions and new ideas? Were they flexible and understanding? Or were they rigid, self-righteous and condemning?

When denial is a major family dynamic, communication styles feature —

- Displays of impatience with what the other person is saying.
- Secretiveness about feelings and activities.
- Diversion away from and distortion of the real issues.
- Interrupting at every opportunity.
- Clinging tenaciously to your own point of view regardless of its merits.
- Trying to make the other person feel stupid or guilty or out of touch.
- Being outwardly agreeable while feeling totally unreceptive on the inside.
- Being critical of others while rejecting criticism of yourself.
- Being self-righteous and blaming about other people's mistakes while ignoring your own wrong-doing.

This style of communication is stultifying, frustrating and distancing. As Barry, a client of mine, said, "Talking to my parents was like talking to a brick wall. They were right and I was wrong. Period. End of conversation." Unfortunately, Barry failed to realize that the biggest influence on our own behavior is the behavior of the parents who raised us. Their communication style becomes our own, as do their habits, beliefs and values. Even the behavior we detest in our parents, we unconsciously take on as our own.

Barry, who was an emergency room physician, originally came to me because of an increasing sense of loneliness, isolation and sense of inadequacy in both his personal and professional lives. Although he was recognized as a highly skilled medical specialist, he was an unpopular member of the hospital staff. The emptiness in his love life he blamed on the grueling demands of his work.

After several months of counseling, Barry and I were making very little progress. He remained defensive and hostile to suggestions for change. My attempts at gentle confrontation were met with intellectual acrobatics and a torrent of 12-syllable words I could understand but not pronounce. At the end of our therapy sessions I frequently felt stupid and inadequate.

I began to feel I was beating my head against a brick wall. *Beating my head against a wall.* That phrase rang a bell.

At our next session I suggested we do some role-switching. He would play me and I would play him. When I looked away from him impatiently and when I imitated his rigid posture and stiff hand and mouth movements, he stopped me in shock.

"You look just like my father!" he said, stunned. "I vowed I'd never be as closed-minded and rejecting as he is. I don't act like that!"

"Yes," I said, "you do. You behave just like your father. Look at how you're turning away from me right now. You practically have your back to me. You turn away whenever I tell you something you don't want to hear. You shut it out completely. You predicate your self-esteem on having to be right all the time. Don't you understand that you don't always have to be perfect in order to have value as a person?"

"You don't understand," he insisted, "a doctor can't afford to make mistakes."

"But you do make mistakes. You can't help it, you're only human. How can you learn anything at all about other people if you're constantly on the defensive — thinking only about your own performance?" As we talked, Barry grudgingly admitted that he might have picked up stand-offishness and defensiveness from his parents.

"But I can be better than they ever were," he said bitterly.

"Yes," I agreed. "You can have a better life. But despite the best of intentions, you keep sabotaging yourself with rigidity and denial. If you want to become a better person, you've got to start by breaking down that thick wall of denial you're protecting yourself with."

Barry hit me with a barrage of poly-syllabic verbiage that went on for quite a few minutes. Then he sighed and said, "Shit." It was a therapeutic breakthrough.

As part of his therapy, I asked Barry to take a searching moral inventory in which he kept a written diary of his closed and stand-offish behaviors.

While it took several weeks, Barry finally came to the conclusion that much of his current unhappiness was of his own making.

"I've been a complete ass," he said disgustedly.

I disagreed. "I think you've been a frightened adult child stuck in denial."

Barry realized that his closed behaviors represented a formidable barrier to change, and if he was to reach his full vitality and potential, he would have to open up emotionally.

He decided that to become the person he wanted to be, he would have to work on three new behaviors. He made this list and brought it to me.

Becoming Emotionally Open

1. Instead of being secretive, I will work daily on being open and honest in my actions and emotions, focusing on the idea that I have nothing to hide.

2. Instead of being defensive, I will work daily on being receptive to the ideas and opinions of other people, focusing on the idea that I don't always have to win.
3. Instead of being self-righteous, I will work daily on being constructively self-critical, focusing on taking responsibility for myself rather than blaming others.

Every morning before he started his workday Barry reinforced his determination by re-reading his list. In the evening he spent about 15 minutes writing a self-report on his day. This helped him to recognize the situations that cued him to close up tight again.

Opening up was not an easy task for Barry. It's not easy for any of us, especially when years of practice make defensiveness almost a reflex action. The following exercise can help you keep an open attitude.

Affirming Openness

Affirmations are a powerful tool for changing negative beliefs and values. By speaking directly to ourselves in a positive and loving manner we can build attitudes which act as a counterbalance to the conditioned reflex of our defensiveness.

Affirmations are done for a few minutes every day, at a regular time or whenever we feel tense or anxious. They can be written, spoken aloud or silently repeated.

The following affirmations are designed particularly to combat a closed emotional stance. Barry used them several times a day for two months.

I, Barry, am open and receptive.
You, Barry, are open and receptive.
Barry is open and receptive.

I, Barry, have value even when I'm wrong.
You, Barry, have value even when you're wrong.
Barry has value even when he's wrong.

I, Barry, am only human.
You, Barry, are only human.
Barry is only human.

Notice that each affirmation takes three forms: An "I" statement; a "you" statement; and a "name" statement. Hearing these statements from three different points of view will help you make these open attitudes a reality. You can use other affirmations as a positive inner voice of strength and courage. For example:

I (Your Name) am confident and strong and happy.
I can face today's challenge.
I feel loved and loving today.
I feel happy and glad to be alive.

7

Paradox 2:
Fear and the Mask
of Invulnerability

We get so much in the habit of wearing a disguise before others that we finally appear disguised before ourselves.

— *La Rochefoucauld*

In our age of technological wonders there's a place where even the most advanced, most finely tuned and calibrated machines can't penetrate. In each of us, inside our deepest emotional selves lives a small child who never grows up. The small child won't show up on a conventional x-ray or a computed tomography (CT) scan. The small inner child remains invisible to the almost-magical probing of nuclear magnetic resonance imaging. Invisible, but ever-present, a part of every cell, every fiber of being.

No matter how big, strong, capable and successful we become, a part of us still feels small and helpless. We are afraid of disapproval, scared of making mistakes, terrified of being found out. We worry about rejection and abandonment. We fear isolation, being left alone to fend for ourselves in a world hostile to us, or worse: utterly indifferent.

At times everyone — not just children of alcoholics — feels like a lost child, stumbling alone in the crowd, sucking his thumb and hoping not to be found out as a fool.

Sadly, this perpetually frightened child feeling is frequently over-developed in people who grow up with alcoholic and co-dependent parents. And is it any wonder?

As a child in an alcoholic home you were bombarded constantly with threats to your physical and emotional safety. You were forced to take on the physical, psychological and social responsibilities of adulthood before you were emotionally prepared to cope with them. And you probably did a fairly decent job of it, too.

But it is scary to a child to take on adult worries, cares and responsibilities. After all, from a child's vantage point, the adult world looks big, powerful and menacing. In comparison, the child is small and powerless. Almost invisible. Without a loving and reliable parent to guide the way, the world seems frightening, overwhelming.

To be sure, alcoholic and co-dependent parents do love their children. Of this there can be no doubt. Neither can we doubt the simple truth that alcoholism turns even the most loving parent into a person who is unreliable, unpredictable, and emotionally distant.

Because alcoholic and co-dependent parents are so wrapped up in their own problems, kids are frequently left to fend for themselves. Even when your parents were in the same room with you, they may have been unavailable to you emotionally.

It's not that you were left alone all the time.

No, it was much worse than that.

You were isolated with a person you couldn't predict, count on or control. You were stuck. You felt trapped in a kind of living hell, damned if you tried to escape and damned if you stayed.

Now think back. Did you talk about your anxiety and fears? Did you openly discuss your sense of insecurity and isolation?

Certainly not!

That would be breaking the rules. Admitting such feelings would be a direct violation of the alcoholic family's conspiracy of silence. Just as your anger had to be denied, so did your fears. You had to be strong, invulnerable, controlled, proud. Those were the rules, the covert laws of the codependent domain.

Those dimly articulated regulations foster the adult child's second paradox: A fragile inner life of fear and anxiety covered by a false front of competence and bravado.

Tanya accurately described this paradox: "I have this feeling of being in over my head all the time. I feel overwhelmed. It's hard to talk about, but it's like I have to please everyone, make everybody think I'm this strong, wonderful person. I feel stuck, always struggling, but never getting to where I want to be."

At the same time Tanya was objective enough to realize that in many ways she was the very image of success. At work she was even considered a role model for some of the younger women — an example of the enterprising woman executive.

"What a joke!" Tanya said ruefully. "I worry all the time that one of these days my mistakes will catch up with me and everyone will find out what I'm really like. Just thinking about it puts me in a depression."

Tanya isn't alone. Her feelings of being overwhelmed, of being stuck, of constantly trying to please are common among adult children. And so is her well-practiced ability to present an image of having it all together. She's really very good at fooling people.

This pretense of emotional invulnerability does not come cheaply. The denial and deceptions needed to hide our real selves from others exact a high cost in terms of lost self-esteem, secret guilt and endless nightmares of inadequacy.

Sadly, when a person has to expend so much energy pretending to be a strong, capable and invulnerable adult when they don't really feel that way, they risk the possibility of forever feeling like a frightened child inside.

Emotionally Stuck In Childhood

All children need and want help in structuring and controlling their lives. In alcoholic families this necessary guidance is either totally missing or confusingly inconsistent. To add insult to injury, the little structure that is provided in alcoholic homes is based on parental needs rather than the needs of the child.

Your mother or father needed you to grow up fast socially and emotionally in order to satisfy their own ego needs. If your family was poor, you may have had to assume early financial responsibilities.

Even if money wasn't a problem, your confused and emotionally inadequate parents may have relied on you to provide emotional support beyond your capabilities, to be a confidante to adult worries, to care for other children, to act as a mini-mother or mini-father. And in some instances, even to act as a mini-spouse.

Your character was prematurely structured into adult-like behaviors, but on the inside you still had the feelings and fears that were appropriate for what you really were: A child.

You were pushed to grow up too fast, you were structured so early to behave in a way that was beyond your emotional limits, that there was little room for further growth and personality development.

As a consequence you became emotionally stuck in a place where you were part child and part adult.

You were a child adult.

Neither fish, nor fowl; neither child, nor adult.

Now, when you are physically grown-up, you may be suffering the stunting emotional effects of premature structuring. Your mature behavior belies the truth — in many ways you still feel like a kid.

If you were forced to grow-up fast to satisfy parental ego needs without concern for your own needs, you will inevitably reach a point of rebellion. You will struggle against the constraints of your existence. You will want to grow, to expand, to find the answers to life's questions.

In agonizing moments of introspection you ask: Is this all there is? Is this enough? And ultimately you cry out in desperation: Who am I — really?!

Where Can You Go?

But what can you do? Where does a man or woman who has been trained from childhood to deny and hide vulnerable feelings go for answers to these deeply personal existential questions? How can you address the deeper issues of your life when to do so raises an irrationally ingrained fear of physical or emotional annihilation?

You can hold tight to your emotions for a long time — some people can hold on forever — but for many adult children of alcoholics, crisis-time hits somewhere in the mid-thirties. It's a natural time to take stock, not just for adult children, but everyone.

We start asking questions: "Where am I going?" "What am I doing?" "Why am I doing it?" And we worry: "Is it ever going to get any better?" "Has life passed me by?"

We want answers to our questions, we want to understand the meaning of our lives. If the answers don't come, we may drop into an emotional tailspin, opening ourselves to anything that provides even temporary relief from our anxiety and questions — alcohol, drugs, food, smoking, work, new lovers, encounter groups, meditation, religious cults.

A voice inside is shouting: *Take stock! When is it going to get better? You've been living somebody else's life. When are you going to start living your own life? Half your life is gone! Is this all there is?*

As one adult child said, "It was like I woke up one day and found out the race was almost over, and I hadn't even left the starting gate."

Confronted with the undeniable reality that you no longer have all the time in the world to find yourself, you are quite simply terrified.

The question is: Do you face your fear head on, or do you run from it?

Do you even possess the necessary emotional equipment required to confront the frightened child inside you? Your parents certainly didn't act as exemplars, as good models, did they?

As a child in an alcoholic home, you were placed under tremendous pressure to solve problems over which you had no control, to please, to make things better without asking questions or making waves or asking for outside help.

You became an active member in the conspiracy of silence, learning that it was important for you to cope without admitting the confusion or pain or fear you felt every time your parents behaved like crazy people with their deceits and moods and unpredictability.

Even though you were only eight or ten years old, you were expected to adjust to problems your parents couldn't handle. You were expected to cope without cracking, to stuff your feelings, to not only survive yourself, but to protect your siblings and help your parents in their struggles.

You weren't up to the task. No child is.

Survival Techniques

So there you were — a child burdened with adult worries but without the grace of adult knowledge. What could you possibly do? Who could you turn to? What were your options?

If you were a normal child living under these chaotic circumstances, you soon learned how to use your own behavior to bring a semblance of order and control to your environment. You learned there were some specific things you could do that made life just a little bit easier to bear . . . if only for the moment.

You learned to lie because sometimes it was the only way to keep the peace.

You learned to manipulate because sometimes it was the only way to obtain the emotional and physical necessities of life.

You learned to tell people what they wanted to hear because sometimes it was the only way to shut them up.

You learned to make promises you couldn't keep because sometimes that was the only way to win approval.

And you learned to hide your emotions because sometimes that was the only way to avoid unbearable pain.

When carried into adulthood, these childhood survival skills become the tools of self-destruction. If we lie, manipulate and pretend in our adult relationships, we end up short-circuiting our capacity to love and be loved. The constant strain of protecting ourselves against detection puts us into a frenzy of fear.

And it makes us feel guilty!

Part of the paradox is that most adult children have pretty high standards of conduct. You aren't a sociopath — you know the difference between right and wrong. And you care about others. When you stretch the truth or withhold information or pretend to be something you're not, you aren't deliberately trying to hurt anyone. You're just trying to get by, keep your self-esteem intact and avoid disaster. And still you hurt.

Because you admire honesty.

Lies, half-truths, pretenses, manipulations and unkept promises violate higher values of integrity, truthfulness, authenticity and personal responsibility.

You want to be honest, but something always gets in the way. You want to learn to be open and above-board, yet the fear of being judged and found wanting prevents you from showing your real self. You want to enjoy the freedoms of adulthood, but you find instead that the old roles and conflicts of childhood reappear to haunt you.

Ask yourself the following questions:

☐ Do you withhold information about your feelings, so the people closest to you have to guess what's really in your mind and heart?

☐ Is it hard for you to make a direct request because being denied makes you feel unloved?

☐ Is it hard for you to tell the people you love how much you really care about them?

☐ Do you worry about keeping track of all the half-truths, misrepresentations and lies you tell to different people?

☐ Do you feel isolated and afraid of people and authority figures?

☐ Do you sometimes feel you have no identity of your own?

☐ Would you rather swallow poison than be publicly exposed as being wrong or unable to competently handle your responsibilities?

☐ When put on the spot, do you become defensive and justify your actions by blaming or criticizing others?

There's a tug-of-war, a bitter conflict, between the desire to fulfill our higher values of honesty and integrity and the need to protect our frightened inner selves with a wall of denial, deceptions and pretense.

This conflict is one of the major sources of our anxiety.

Understanding this anxiety is one of our most important tasks. Our self-esteem is based in large part on this most fundamental human dilemma — do we live up to our higher values or do we play to our fears?

To be honest or to be safe? Which will it be? As children we had no way of knowing there were other modes of operating. We lied because we had to. We manipulated and pretended because it helped us get by. It didn't make us happy, just safe for a minute or two. We simply did what had to be done to survive.

But as adults we stand on the crossroads of choice, all possibilities open to us.

In all honesty it must be said again that the path to taming a turbulent past is not an easy one to follow.

For if we choose to pursue our higher values, if we pick openness and honesty and integrity, then we must forsake our mask of invulnerability. We must stand naked and be judged for who and what we really are.

And that's what terrifies us.

8

Fear:
A Zero State

Fear is a slinking cat I find
Beneath the lilacs of my mind.

— *Sophie Tunnell*

Although fear may manifest itself in a thousand and one ways, the adult child's basic fear is that "deep down inside, I am nothing."

Zero.

Because we fear the emptiness inside, we don't look inward. It's too scary. Inside us there is a deep and pervasive feeling of badness. It is not intellectual, it is emotional. It is in our very guts, the feeling that, "I am nothing". So we project a made-up image to the world, a picture we hope is pleasing. And we allow no one to see inside. It feels safer that way.

We struggle daily to keep our projected image intact. *But because this image is phony, it produces fear.*

The image we project seems sturdy, but it's really very fragile, like a thin glass globe containing clouds and shadowy figures. An illusion. And like the fragile glass globe, our image can be shattered in many ways. A friend's cross remark, a co-worker's criticism, a lover's momentary indifference. Each of these small acts has in it the power to shatter our confidence. So we guard ourselves the best way we know how, by placing a protective mask over our emotions.

We so carefully conceal our inner anxieties that even our closest friends are usually unaware of their pervasive nature.

To a certain extent this makes sense. Without some degree of outward poise, we'd never be able to sit through a job interview or walk into a room full of people or carry on a casual conversation with a stranger. If we put every twinge of our inner anxiety on display for all the world to see, we would soon be labeled nut cases.

Obviously a certain amount of concealment is beneficial. But too often our mask of invulnerability cuts us off from love and growth and positive change. It traps us, keeping us isolated and alone even while we are in the company of those we love.

The anxiety, however, remains. It stays inside us and incubates, growing monstrous and savage, something to be dreaded, pushed away, destroyed.

Anxiety becomes our enemy, an inhibiting, paralyzing force . . .

. . . fear of ridicule, rejection, humiliation
. . . fear of failure, defeat, loss
. . . fear of being unloved, lost, abandoned
. . . fear of weakness, discovery, vulnerability
. . . and fear of fear itself.

Ramifications of Fear

In particular, the adult child gets trapped by fear of physical injury, pain and possible death. This fear is over-developed, far beyond the normal reluctance any person has to avoid pain. A trip to the doctor or dentist for minor procedures becomes an ordeal of terror accompanied by the expectation of major pain, mutilation or maiming.

The result? Very often relatively minor medical and dental problems develop into major illnesses. A simple case of tooth decay, through avoidance, turns into a root canal job. A minor cut, through neglect, turns into a major infection.

Brenda learned about the ramifications of fear the hard way. She ignored irregular vaginal bleeding for months because she couldn't stand the thought of undergoing the terrible pain of a pelvic exam and pap test.

Under normal circumstances, a routine pelvic exam can be uncomfortable and embarrassing, but it is not physically painful. Still, Brenda's fear of the procedure prevented her from making a doctor's appointment. But there was more to it than that.

Brenda wasn't stupid — she'd read the seven warning signs of cancer. Unusual bleeding, that was one of them. No way was she going to let them cut her up and make her hair fall out and stick her full of drainage tubes. If she was going to die, she'd rather do it fast, make it look like an accident, not waste away like some vegetable in a hospital bed.

She kept hoping the bleeding would stop on its own. It didn't. Home alone in the middle of the night, Brenda suffered a life-threatening uterine hemorrhage.

It wasn't cancer. Her doctor told her that had she sought medical care months earlier, her common problem could have been taken care of with a simple office procedure under local anesthetic. Instead Brenda ended up with major surgery, weeks of convalescence and a huge medical bill.

It would be easy, even comforting, to dismiss Brenda as an oddball, a foolish woman with an overactive imagination and an appalling lack of common sense. Easy, but not helpful.

Brenda doesn't fit the stereotype. She is an intelligent and capable woman with a strong desire to lead a happy, normal life. But, she finds herself handicapped by omnipresent fears — the adult child's legacy from a childhood of shame and confusion, lies and cover-ups, wild hopes and bitter disappointments.

Like Brenda, many adult children allow legitimate small worries to snowball in their minds into major catastrophes. A friend of mine named Loni calls this process negative intuition.

Negative Intuitions and Catastrophic Fantasies

As Loni described it to me over lunch one day, "Whenever anything even a little bit bad happens, I start imagining the very worst. For instance, a few months ago I found a picture of my husband, Todd, with his arm around a woman he works with. She's very beautiful, tall and slim and young. I was devastated."

Loni confronted her husband with the picture and after several days of arguing, Todd finally convinced her that the young woman in the picture meant nothing to him. He assured Loni repeatedly that he loved her and was committed to their marriage. And Loni believed him.

But her negative intuitions wouldn't let her rest. Todd was a very good looking man. She suspected that young girls might find him attractive. And that began to worry her.

"I'd look in the mirror," she recalled, "and I'd see lines on my face I hadn't seen before. I started thinking that I was getting older. I'm 34 and I've had a child. My body isn't as firm as it used to be and each year it seems I gain a pound or two. How long would it be before Todd found me too old and fat? How long until he left me for one of the beautiful, nubile girls he works with?"

Loni's imagination began to run wild. "I saw myself deserted, divorced, poor and too ugly for any other man to want. I cried myself to sleep worrying about it."

Loni finally snapped herself out of the corrosive welter of negative intuitions and catastrophic fantasies by keeping a journal where she recorded her fears on one side of the page and the positive realities on the other. Her journal looked like this:

JOURNAL

Fears:	Positive Realities:
I'm turning into a pathetic old woman.	I'm only 34 years old and nowadays that's still young.
I'm fat and ugly.	I weigh 12 lbs. more than I did when Todd married me. That's only one dress size.
No one will ever love me again if I lose Todd.	I'm not going to lose Todd. But if I do, I'll find love again. I'll still be lovable.
I can't support myself without Todd's help.	I have a college education and good job experience. It might be hard, but I could support myself if I had to.

Every time Loni felt a surge of catastrophic fantasies taking over, she opened up her journal and forced herself to look at her fear rationally. By concentrating on the positive realities of her life, she was able to get on with the important business of living each day fully and she was also able to openly accept Todd's affection and assurances of his love.

Several months later Loni laughed and blushed as she told me about the way her negative intuitions had sent her into a tailspin of fear. "You know, I actually had myself half convinced I was going to end up a Bag Lady. All because of that stupid picture."

Catastrophic Fantasies of Abandonment

Loni's experience illustrates one of the adult child's most common catastrophic fantasies — the deep inner fear of being abandoned by those we love.

Abandonment, physical and emotional, is a reality in alcoholic homes. Alcoholic fathers are frequently autocratic and unreasonable in their demands. They view themselves as always right and anyone who fails to live up to their standards as always wrong.

Co-dependent mothers repeatedly emphasize how responsible, put-upon, correct and hardworking they are. They have you believing they are always considerate and always thinking of your needs first. They can't understand why you are so inconsiderate and selfish in return. Why do you insist on hurting them with your every action?

Young children — believing as children do in the infallibilty of their parents — begin to think of themselves as bad, unworthy and the cause of their parents' problems.

Of course, this is nonsense. But how is a child to know that?

Children frequently come to believe it is their own badness that makes Daddy drink, makes Mommy miserable, makes Daddy slam out the door and stay away for hours and hours.

If only I was better . . . if I was a better child . . . if I was a perfect child . . . then my Mommy and Daddy would be happy, they would love me and everything would be better . . . if only I wasn't so bad . . .

How does a child cope with so heavy a burden? How does a child survive the invisible stigmata of complete badness in a universe where everyone else is so worthy and right and perfect?

If only I was a perfect child . . .

The Perfect Disguise

No matter how hard we try, perfection is beyond our human ability. But we can put on a front, we can present an image of goodness and perfection. It's possible to act "as if" . . .

- I don't make mistakes
- I don't have hateful thoughts
- I don't have deep inner fears
- I don't feel inadequate
- I don't behave badly
- I don't hurt
- I don't care

It's possible to act as if . . . *I am invulnerable.*

The child comes to believe that not an ounce of fear or weakness can be displayed . . . all must be perfect. I mustn't show my real self, the child reasons. *The real me is bad and unworthy and unlovable. The real me would be abandoned.*

In this way the child learns to wear a mask before others. The masks take various forms:

One mask gives the appearance of goodness, sweetness and light. By behaving in this way, the child hopes to win the approval of the all-powerful, always-right parent.

Another mask allows the child to blend into the background like a chameleon hoping to attract as little attention as possible. The chameleon seeks safety by being inconspicuous.

A third mask presents an image of toughness and brusque invulnerability. Leave me alone, this mask warns. Don't question my actions.

Still another mask is the face of indifference. Pretending not to care at all covers the pain of caring so much.

Our protective masks create a vicious circle. Because we fear abandonment, we withhold the authentic nature of our real selves; and because we withhold our real feelings, we create distance and loneliness in our relationships; and because we are so distant and uncommunicative with our loved ones, they become rejecting and angry with us.

Because we fear abandonment, we act like jerks. And because we act like jerks, we are abandoned.

The circle is complete.

Simon, a 35-year-old attorney, explained why he wouldn't tell Laura, his live-in partner of three years, that he loved her. "I don't want to make that kind of commitment," he told me. "I don't want her to have that kind of power over me. I feign indifference so much that I've got used to it. Maybe I'm missing out on a lot of warmth and tenderness, like you say, but maybe I'm missing a lot of pain, too."

Underneath his air of detachment, Simon sounded very sad when we talked about his sense of loneliness, fear and isolation.

"In my family," he said, "you wore a mask over your real feelings. If you showed you were upset or scared or worried, the picking started. 'What's wrong with you?' 'Wipe that ugly look off your face!' 'Don't be a cry-baby.' Pick, pick, pick. As far as I'm concerned, it's a hell of a lot safer to keep my feelings to myself. The less people know about what's going on inside me, the safer I feel."

Like Simon, many adult children dare not risk exposure of their real feelings because they fear being hurt, manipulated, rejected, ridiculed or humiliated.

Simon also used his profession as a rationalization for his aloofness. "Clients don't trust a tax attorney who's emotionally labile," he said. "I have to be in control at all times."

He couldn't explain how expressing affection for the woman he loved would hurt his legal career, yet he still possessed a deep-seated belief that any show of emotional vulnerability would be irreparably harmful to him.

On the surface Simon's coldness makes him sound like a stubborn fool who deserves every bit of loneliness that comes his way. But if we realize that Simon, at age 35, is just now beginning to acknowledge the unresolved conflicts he feels about his father's alcoholism, perhaps we can be less harsh in our judgment.

An alcoholic family is not a safe place to show honest emotion. Too often, tender displays are trampled on by parents who are too drugged or troubled to respond sensitively. If your childhood expressions of vulnerability were met with ridicule, anger or judgments, you may have felt too frightened and assaulted to risk exposing yourself again.

Sharing true feelings was dangerous because you could never predict how your turbulent parents would respond. Naturally, you did what you had to do to protect your emotional self.

Simon puts it this way, "I have to stay in control. There will be no messy disclosures of my true feelings, no displays of weakness, no opportunity to be hurt and embarrassed. That's the way I am, and if Laura doesn't like it . . . well, that's too bad."

And it is too bad — too bad for Laura because she has no way of knowing Simon's real feelings. But mostly too bad for

Simon because it means he's living an emotionally-constricted life. He sought counseling because he knew something was missing in his relationships. It never occurred to him that what was missing was the real Simon. Think about your own life. Are you caught in the same kind of trap? Are you allowing a facade of strength to keep you weak and frightened? Are you hiding behind a mask of invulnerability?

THE INVULNERABLE ADULT CHILD

We are not invulnerable; we are closed, rigid, frozen.
We are not strong; we are too frightened to show our weakness.
We are not safe; we are merely hiding.

9

Avoiding the Pitfall of Perfectionism

Lord, grant me the serenity to do what I can do, to give it my best shot and to be reasonably satisfied if it doesn't come out perfect.

— *Recovering Perfectionist's Prayer*

D r. David Burns, founder of the Behavioral Sciences Research Foundation, dares emotional perfectionists to attempt a new and perhaps audacious challenge: Try being average. At first glance this idea sounds totally absurd, for who in their right mind would strive for such a boring, ordinary level of achievement? It takes no special effort to be mediocre.

But wait. Upon reflection it seems to me that Dr. Burns is on to something wonderful here. Because as he points out, if you are a perfectionist, you are bound to be a loser at whatever you do. A consummate failure. A sublime flop.

A perfectionist will always fail to meet the elevated standards of perfection. If examined with a critical eye, everything, every person, every idea falls short of perfection. Only in the movies was Bo Derek a "10". And even there the critics ranked her acting "3" or below.

Likewise, every achievement falls short of perfection. It can be fixed up, honed, modified, fine-tuned and tinkered with in some way to make it "better".

When you pursue perfection, you will inevitably run headlong into frustration, self-hate and misery. Yet if you are willing to walk down the road of "averageness" for even one day, you are bound to feel successful, accomplished and pleased with yourself because maybe for the first time in your life you will be striving for an attainable goal. Finally, you can succeed.

How To Be An Anti-perfectionist

Our perfectionistic tendency is usually so ingrained that it has become an unthinking emotional reflex for us. Breaking our reflexive responses takes both effort and practice. On the following pages I will describe several exercises that have proven effective in helping other adult children overcome the feelings of anxiety produced by their emotional perfectionism.

Set aside some time to do these exercises, remembering that the heavier your burden of perfection, the more practice you'll need to learn the joys of imperfection.

Anti-perfection Exercise 1: Doing It Right.

If you are a perfectionist, you are undoubtedly an expert at negative self-talk. If you are in any way typical, it's likely that you lie in bed at night going over everything you did wrong today. You know how to focus on the areas where you fall short. You catalogue every mistake, blunder and clumsy encounter. Why did you say this? Why didn't you say that? Did they like you? Why did they give you that funny look? And on and on. You fall asleep counting your shortcomings instead of sheep. No wonder you feel anxious.

Tonight try something different. When your mind starts racing with negativity, say to yourself, "NO! Not now. I'm not going to dwell on the negative." This is a technique called thought stopping, and it works.

Now after you have ordered yourself to stop your negative self-talk, substitute at least five minutes of positive self-talk. What did you do right today? How many things can you count that are positive? Pay special attention to the little things you just normally expect of yourself.

At first your perfectionistic negativity may be so automatic, so ingrained and habitual, that you can't think of a single thing you did right. But you probably did a lot of good things that you take for granted, like getting to work on time, passing up that second piece of chocolate cake, making a dreaded phone call, being patient with a rude store clerk, and so on. You don't need to score big. We want you to appreciate yourself for all the good ordinary normal things you accomplish in a day.

The purpose of this exercise is to break your emotional reflex of negative self-appraisal. If negativity creeps in, say "NO! Not now!" and continue giving yourself positive feedback.

Now this doesn't mean that you should never again critique your behavior for areas that need improvement. We all need to do that occasionally. But we perfectionists get carried away with the habit. What we really need practice on is patting ourselves on the back a little bit for all the things we usually take for granted.

This exercise will be most effective if you practice it at least five minutes a night over a period of weeks. It takes time to replace the habit of negative self-appraisal with the habit of positive self-appraisal. Remember that, because your perfectionistic reflex will make you want to become an expert in positive self-talk in just one night!

Anti-perfection Exercise 2: Less is More

Like many perfectionists you may believe that producing anything less than definitive work is just about the same as producing garbage. You feel deeply shamed if even small flaws are detected in what you do. Such feelings invariably lead to (1) burn-out from trying to do everything perfectly, or (2) emotional and mental paralysis from the prospect of facing the impossible.

Here's an experiment suggested by Dr. Burns: Try changing your standards with various activities to see how your performance responds to high, middle and low standards. I've tried this with my writing, my counseling and with dieting, and I've been very pleasantly surprised with the outcome whenever I have lowered my standards. I end up producing more and feeling better about myself.

For example, when I started writing the section on fear for this book, I thought I should cover every aspect of fear, from anxiety disorders through agoraphobia, traumatic stress disorder and obsessive-compulsive behavior. Now, let's see, what did I leave out? Oh, yes. I should outline all of the latest behavioral and cognitive research in addition to addressing the bio-chemistry and genetics of anxiety. And that was just for starters. I also decided I should write at least 10 manuscript pages a day.

I would cover the field so thoroughly that I would qualify for an honorary degree in fear.

At one point, the workspace around my computer was so laden with piles of notes and clippings and reference materials that I couldn't find the keyboard. At that moment I developed writer's block.

My perfectionism had thwarted me.

I decided to lower my standards. Each day I made it my goal to cover a little less material and instead of aiming for 10 pages a day, I aimed for one. This meant that I could accomplish my goal easily. I felt so good about this that I was spurred on to write more, knowing that each new paragraph was more than I had hoped for.

When my standards were high — 10 pages a day — I failed consistently. I felt bad about myself and even considered giving up the project completely. The minute I lowered my standard, I started feeling like a success again. And over a period of days the manuscript pages piled up until the chapters were done.

Since that time I have never abandoned my aim of doing less each day. Consequently I never feel frustrated or inadequate. I feel good because I am achieving my goal and that motivates me to continue.

Try Dr. Burns' suggestion and dare to be average. When you start a project, lower your sights. Instead of aiming for 110%, go for 50% or 30% or even 10% like I did. Then see if you don't enjoy yourself and become more productive at the same time.

Anti-perfection Exercise 3:
Making Mistakes

Here's a contradiction for you — emotional perfectionists are unrelentingly self-critical, yet we'll be dipped in hot tar before we'll take responsibility for our own mistakes.

There's a psychological reason for this. The knowledge that we have behaved badly or foolishly or with a mean spirit gives our self-image a brutal jarring. How can we be the perfectly wonderful person we're supposed to be and make all these stupid blunders?

Psychologists call this conflict between perception and reality "cognitive dissonance." The human psyche just cannot tolerate such mental discrepancies — anxiety and panic attacks are frequent manifestations of cognitive dissonance in process.

How do we humans resolve this intolerable dissonance in our perceptions? It's really quite simple. We, consciously or unconsciously, redefine reality to meet our needs.

Either we accept the fact that we are not always perfect and wonderful or we maintain our self-image by throwing the blame for our mistakes on someone or something else.

- "It was the secretary's fault that the budget and annual report didn't get finished in time for the site visit."

- "I coulda been a contender." (But I didn't get the right breaks, know the right people, have the right connections, etc.)
- "I didn't get all "A's" my senior year because my math instructor knew I had a high grade average and he was out to get me."
- "I could have been a success if my father wasn't an alcoholic."

Unless we've done quite a bit of work to overcome our perfectionist tendencies, you can bet we'll opt for maintaining our emotional illusions.

So while we may moan more or less incessantly about our problems, burdens and difficulties in life, we emotional perfectionists are loath to honestly and truly take responsibility for our lapses in perfection. Oh, we hurl insults at ourselves, but that's not an effective way of admitting specific mistakes. Sometimes we even criticize ourselves in order to take the sting out of criticism from others.

Sadly, if we are unable to admit our errors, we have also cut off our ability to grow and change.

Consciously analyzing the irrational and self-defeating nature of our belief in the importance of perfection is one way of facing the transcendental truth that "to err is human".

Using your journal, write a list in which you outline why a fear of making mistakes is detrimental to you. How does attempting to maintain a self-image of perfection inhibit your potential for growth? Valerie's journal looked like this:

Why It's Okay For Me To Make Mistakes

1. First, it's okay for me to make mistakes because all humans make mistakes. Thinking that I can be perfect is grandiose and irrational — why should I be immune from the laws of humanity?
2. Making mistakes is okay because I learn from them. When I refuse to accept my mistakes, I become rigid and unable to improve myself.
3. It's okay to be less than perfect because one small flaw doesn't ruin an otherwise good outcome. A 98% success

rate with peace of mind is better than 100% success with a nervous breakdown.

4. If I recognize where I messed up, I can change it. The discomfort of admitting I've goofed will be worth it if I can make a positive change that will make me happier in the long run.

5. Whenever I try to do 110% perfect job, I either get burned out from the strain or I get so paralyzed from anxiety that I want to hide under my bed. Then I start procrastinating. When I lower my standards to 90%, I get more done.

6. It's okay to make a mistake because it makes me more human. Most people won't hold small mistakes against me. And I think sometimes my pretense of perfection puts other people off.

7. Lastly, even if I really blow it and a lot of people get mad at me and criticize me, I won't die from it. I will feel bad for a while, but if I honestly admit my mistakes I can make amends to the people I hurt and forgive myself. It won't be the end of the world.

Rationally analyzing mistake-making does not guarantee you emotional relief, but it is a start. Valerie reported a large decrease in her feelings of anxiety and fear immediately after writing her essay. However, about a month later her perfectionist tendencies burst forth again when she had to present a proposal to her boss and co-workers. A panic attack struck as she was going over last minute details.

"I thought 'this is the end'," she recalled. Then I said, 'NO!' I sat down at my desk and did some slow deep breathing and mentally I recited all the reasons why I didn't have to be perfect. I remembered my list of why it was okay for me to make mistakes, and gradually my panic left me. My heart-beat slowed to normal; the lump left my throat; I was okay. I went to the lady's room and wiped the sweat off my face and body, all the time saying to myself, 'It's okay to make mistakes. My self-worth does not depend on making a perfect presentation.' Then I went into the meeting room and knocked 'em dead! My legs felt like Jello, but, dammit! I did it!"

After that, Valerie practiced this exercise regularly, especially before any situation where she felt her skills and abilities would be tested and judged.

"I still get nervous," she admits, "but I haven't had to take a Valium in six months."

Using Drugs
To Treat Fear and Anxiety

As Valerie's comment indicates, she had at times turned to prescription medication to deal with her anxiety attacks. Is this an avenue other adult children who suffer from severe fear problems need to explore?

In my opinion, the answer is a qualified "maybe".

Current research shows that some major anxiety disorders may be biochemical — that is, physical, rather than psychological — in origin.

Some people may possess nervous systems that for unknown physical reasons stay on red alert when they should be at ease.

Some researchers are investigating the possibility that a predisposition to a red alert nervous system is a genetic trait which can be passed on from generation to generation. We already know this is true of alcoholism, and it is my personal (unscientific) belief that in the coming years scientists will discover a genetic link between alcoholism and a predisposition to a red alert nervous system.

In other words, I'm saying that children of alcoholics may be hit with a double whammy — the destructive effects of growing up in a dysfunctional family and the possibility of inheriting a nervous system predisposed to anxiety.

Please note, I said may. Even if a link is found, we must remember that not every child in a family inherits the same genes, just as not every child reacts the same way to family chaos. Some children may be severely affected, while others escape unscathed.

So the question remains. Are psycho-active medications a viable option for adult children suffering from fear disorders?

According to psychologist Carol Tavris, "The drugs currently most in use for treating anxiety disorders are the benzodiazepines (minor tranquilizers, such as Valium), tricyclic antidepressants, such as imipramine, and monamine oxidase (MAO) inhibitors, such as phenalazine."

I remain unalterably opposed to the use of benzodiazepines (minor tranquilizers) by adult children of alcoholics except in emergency situations under the direct supervision of a medical person.

Why such a strong stand?

Reason 1: These drugs have a high potential for abuse and addiction.

Reason 2: Adult children of alcoholics have a high potential for all forms of chemical dependency and abuse.

I have seen too many adult children who would never dream of getting drunk or using illegal drugs become physical and emotional wrecks from using legally prescribed tranquilizers. They had no intention of abusing these drugs, yet they still developed serious problems.

It is my deepest conviction that for adult children, the risks of using tranquilizers far outweigh the potential benefits.

And it is the adult child's responsibility to make this point clear to well-meaning physicians who seek to alleviate your suffering by offering you a prescription for any of the many different brands of tranquilizers. To protect yourself, it is vital that you not accept a prescription for an anti-anxiety drug or a muscle relaxant or a sleeping pill without first obtaining from your doctor a complete explanation of exactly what kind of drug you are getting.

Don't be afraid to question either your doctor or your pharmacist. Any doctor worth his (or her) salt will gladly answer your questions. While it is the doctor's responsibility to give you information, it is your responsibility to ask questions if the information isn't freely offered in terms you can understand. Don't feel shy, for you are certainly worth the effort it takes to ask these questions.

Now, what about the tricyclic anti-depressants and the MAO inhibitors? In my experience, under certain conditions, these drugs can be a boon to anxious and depressed adult children of alcoholics. One reason they seem useful is because they pose a lower risk for abuse, mostly because they don't have an euphoric drug effect. In other words, they don't make you high. You might consider being evaluated for drug treatment by a qualified physician if you can answer yes to any of the following questions.

1. Are you unable to carry out your day-to-day activities because of your fear and depression?
2. Do you suffer a lot from physical symptoms such as agitation, racing heart, or feelings of paralysis?
3. Do you have a past history of positive drug treatment with few side effects?

The above guidelines are general in nature and are not meant to be comprehensive. If you do decide to seek medical help, it's important that you know that these drugs often need several weeks to take effect. Sometimes the dosage has to be adjusted several times before optimum benefit is reached. And sometimes the drugs simply don't work for your particular problem.

Without exception, people being treated with drug therapy must stay in close contact with their physician. If the medication doesn't seem to work or if you suffer from side effects, let your doctor know. Otherwise you won't receive the help you want and need.

Self-Medication and Self-Sabotage

Anxiety is a terrible thing.

This is an important truth we can't ignore. Anxiety feels terrible. We'll do just about anything to escape it. We'll medicate ourselves with alcohol, marijuana, pills borrowed from a friend, a pint of Haagen-Daz and two packs of cigarettes.

And that's one of the reasons why counseling, exercises, medication, and insight oftimes don't work to alleviate our pain.

Our lifestyle habits can keep us in misery! Recent research shows that even small amounts of caffeine or sugar can trigger full-blown panic attacks in susceptible people.

Hypoglycemia — low blood sugar — can mimic all the symptoms of mental illness.

Chemical dependency undermines health and happiness.

Constant striving after success and achievement leads to physical exhaustion and emotional burnout.

Stress deadens our emotions and sickens our bodies.

No matter how much we struggle and search and suffer in our quest for self, we will find no lasting happiness if we examine our psyches under a microscope while ignoring the needs of our bodies. Insight is a precious thing, yet it is only a small fragment in the complex puzzle of self-realization. If we spend all our time looking into our emotions while remaining unaware of our physical selves, we stay fragmented. True self-realization comes from wholeness. And fundamental to wholeness is the issue of self-care.

10

Paradox 3: Self-Neglect While Taking Care of Others

First cast out the beam from thine own eye; and then thou shalt see clearly to cast out the mote from thy brother's eye.

— *Matthew 8:5*

I f you ever attend a conference for adult children of alcoholics, you'll soon discover that the vast majority of people there are professional care-givers — nurses, teachers, counselors, social workers, doctors, probation officers, psychologists, health professionals, community volunteers and so on.

This is no coincidence.

Those who have studied the dynamics of the alcoholic family frequently comment on the tendency of children of alcoholics to grow into what are called natural helpers.

Natural helpers are nurturers and problem-solvers and care-givers. They are the men and women who coach little league, and organize bake sales, and sit with you in the emergency room waiting area while your child is having his brain scanned. Natural helpers open their doors to weeping friends at midnight, loan money when they have an overdue notice from the electric company in their own pocket and willingly tolerate personal inconvenience if it means another person will benefit from the sacrifice.

Not surprisingly, natural helpers gravitate toward careers that allow them to utilize their natural talents and inclinations for helping other people — counselor, social worker, doctor, nurse, teacher, lawyer, police officer.

Why shouldn't adult children be drawn to occupations where they can use the skills they developed in surviving the crucible of parental alcoholism? After all, children who grow up in alcoholic homes have ample opportunity to learn the basics:

- How to soothe and calm crazy, unpredictable people
- How to negotiate peace in a war zone
- How to stretch limited resources
- How to find solutions to insoluble problems
- How to prevent unavoidable disaster
- How to please unpleasable (and often unpleasant) people
- How to keep an irrevocably broken down system running
- And how to work that system for all it's worth . . .

And — after all the glamour is stripped away — aren't these the very same skills one needs to effectively provide services to people who are sick or needy or simply uncertain of which direction to go?

Yes, we all know about the importance of displaying empathy, non-possessive warmth, emotional authenticity and expert knowledge. But we also know and understand the conflicts and strife involved in office politics, hospital power struggles and agency warfare.

And when you combine a genuine desire to help other people with the adult child's natural instincts for surviving in a stressed-out, ego-jungle, Cracker Factory atmosphere, what you come up with is a super people-worker. However, just because there seems to be a natural tendency in adult children to gravitate toward the helping professions, it does not mean this tendency will always be a positive and healing force for the adult child or for the people who ask for his or her help.

Wanting To Help
Is Not Always Healthy

According to the National Association of Children of Alcoholics these are some of the characteristics adult children have in common due to growing up in an alcoholic household:

* *We have an overdeveloped sense of responsibility, and it is easier for us to be concerned with others rather than for ourselves.*

* *We live life from the viewpoint of helping and seeking victims, and we are attracted by that weakness in our love and friendship relationships.*

* *We confuse love with pity and tend to "love" people we can pity and rescue.*

* *We judge ourselves harshly and have a very low sense of self-esteem (sometime compensated for by trying to appear superior).*

* *We are dependent personalities who are terrified of abandonment . . .*

The Association states clearly that these words are a description, not an indictment. Yet if I tell you that I can look back at my early years as a counselor trainee and see myself indicted by those words, will you judge me harshly?

If I tell you that I can look around me now and see five, ten, more than a dozen of my professional colleagues hiding their fear and pathology behind a wall of diplomas and certificates and important-sounding titles, will you think me overly-critical?

If I ask you to honestly consider your own motivations for helping other people either as a professional care-giver or amateur natural helper, will you like what you see?

Under close examination the giving behavior of the natural helper does not always look selfless and caring. When adult children give, too often we are —

— Taking care of others while ignoring our own needs.

— Surrounding ourselves with weak and dependent people so we can feel needed, powerful and superior.

— Making people dependent on us in order to quell our omnipresent fear of abandonment.

— Bolstering our self-esteem by do-gooding and glory-seeking.

— Rescuing other people from their problems while our own lives are falling apart from lack of maintenance and repair.

Now is the time for each of use to ask ourselves if our giving, helping, care-taking behavior is simply another mask we wear. Just whose weaknesses, dependencies and needs are we catering to anyway?

In order to really be genuine, warm and empathetic in our interaction with other people — in other words, to be able to really give — we must be relaxed and nondefensive, have our own needs met and have emotional and physical vitality. These conditions imply a kind of emotional and physical harmony, self-awareness, self-care and assertiveness that are alien in alcoholic homes. Children growing up in alcoholic homes simply don't learn from their parents how to take care of their own basic needs in a healthy and positive way.

We learn how to deaden our awareness, ignore our needs, drive ourselves onward, bury our pain and keep on giving to others until we collapse from lack of self-maintenance.

This is the adult child's third paradox: A lifestyle of self-neglect combined with a compelling need to improve the lives of others.

The Glorification of Self-Neglect

Despite 20 years of progress towards a more egalitarian society, modern American women still tend to be the nurturers while men still think of themselves as providers. Even though over 50% of married women hold down full-time jobs, they still do most of the housework.

This is as true in alcoholic families as in any other family. And it is in the role of either nurturer or provider that the daughters and sons of alcoholics live out the third paradox, the paradox of self-neglect.

PARADOX 3

Adult children tend to neglect their own most basic physical and emotional needs. They often justify this self-destructive behavior by saying they are too busy taking care of other people to worry about themselves.

Take Isaac, for example. In his determination to provide for his family, Isaac practiced self-neglect to such a degree he almost left them without a father and husband.

"I wanted my wife and kids to have all the good things I'd missed as a child," he told me. "I wanted the big house with the spa and imported cars and a horse for my daughter. That girl is pure horse-crazy! I didn't want them to feel inferior like I did as a child because they didn't have the right kind of clothes. I didn't want them to be ashamed of the old man."

Of course, such things require money. Lots of it. In addition to his job as a hospital administrator, he started a consulting business on the side. This ambitious project required hours and hours of high-energy work. As did his regular job. Soon Isaac was working 16 hour days, every day. He didn't have time to eat regular meals, and although exhausted, he couldn't sleep at night. He asked one of the doctors at the hospital for some sleeping pills, which he started taking nightly. His wife, Gloria, become both worried and angry. Isaac no longer had the time or energy to relate to his family.

"She'd nag at me," Isaac recalls, "and it made me furious. I was doing it all for her and the kids and the selfish bitch didn't even appreciate it."

Gloria adds, "I kept telling him I needed a husband more than I needed a new car, but he wouldn't listen."

This pattern continued for two years, during which time Isaac grew more and more distant from Gloria and his two children. Then Isaac got sick. It started out as a cold. Isaac ignored it and kept on going . . . until he collapsed three weeks later in the halls of his own hospital.

"I almost died," he says. "I had pneumonia and a viral inflammation of the heart. I'd been sick for almost a month and I'd let it go, which is pretty stupid behavior in a hospital administrator."

How had he rationalized such stupidity? "I told myself I had to keep going for the sake of my family. They were counting on me and I couldn't let them down."

The doctors warned Isaac that if he wanted to avoid permanent heart damage, he'd have to slow down, rest and give his body time to heal. Grudgingly, Isaac agreed to discontinue his consulting business, which meant he'd lose about a third of his income.

Isaac and Gloria sat down with the kids to explain that Daddy had been very sick and in order for him to get well, they'd all have to give up some of the things they liked. "But Daddy's worth it, isn't he?" Gloria prompted.

"Does this mean I have to give up my horse?" nine-year-old Kimberly asked sulkily. "Because if it does, it's not one bit fair!"

"That was a knife in my heart," Isaac says quietly. "The damn horse meant more to my daughter than I did, and it was my own fault. I wasn't a real person to her. What kind of father had I been? I was hardly ever home and when I was, I was tired and irritable. Just like my father had been with me. Suddenly all my rationalizations crashed around me. Doing it for them. It was a lie. I hadn't done anything for them. It had all been for me, so I could feel like a big man, respected, a success. Providing my family with the best of everything was for my own ego glorification, not theirs. Oh, sure, they enjoyed all my material success. But if I'd really been interested in what was best for them, I would have given them some of my time and affection as well as my money. What kind of person was my daughter growing up to be? I had no idea. We were strangers."

Isaac, like many adult children, had confused the trappings of a happy family life — a nice home, abundant food, fashionable clothes, the best schools — with the substance of a happy family — which is love, mutual caring, trust and emotional as well as physical support.

This is a mistake made by many sons of alcoholics —

• Peter brought his weekly paycheck from the mill home and handed it to his wife. He did it because he loved her, and that's the same reason he signed on for double shifts. Yet, in seven years of marriage he had said the words "I love you" only once. And he'd never once complimented his wife for her accomplishments or kindnesses.

• Scott supported his wife's desire to have a career. He showed his support by taking every opportunity to critique her performance, clothes and poise. "I want her to succeed," he explained, "and she can't do that unless she knows where to improve herself. I criticize her because I care about her."

These men are not uncaring louts. They all believe they are operating in the best interest of their loved ones. Yet if that's true, why do their wives feel isolated, neglected and unloved? Why do these men have to keep searching for an impossible and unknown magic something to give meaning to their lives? Why do they neglect and ignore their most basic needs for emotional and physical nourishment, rest, relaxation and connectedness with the people they love? What in the name of heaven is wrong with them?

I have only one answer: They don't know how else to behave. Or if they do know how to behave differently, that knowledge is overridden by the inertia of years of habit, years of thoughtless action and reaction in rigid social roles taken as immutable personality traits.

Isaac, Peter and Scott are re-enacting scenes from their own unhappy childhoods. Scott had endured years of parental criticism, Peter had never heard compliments or words of affection, Isaac had been taught that a real man keeps going, come hell or high water.

Had it made them happy when their parents had acted in these ways? Not on your life! Yet with barely a conscious thought to what they were doing, they continually repeated the melodrama of their turbulent past, and they continued to feel the same self-doubt and unhappiness they had known as children.

They lived as pre-programmed automatons, not as fully alive, emotionally complex human beings.

Women Are Better At This Than Men Are, Right?

Not necessarily. Woman usually cope differently than men, but different doesn't always mean better.

While sons are learning to ignore and discount both internal and external emotional signals, daughters of alcoholics are learning to cope with family turbulence by developing an acute sensitivity to the whims and desires of the people around them. By anticipating the moods and behavior of her unpredictable parents, a girl gains a sense of mastery and control over her environment. Yet in no way does this teach the girl about her own need to be nurtured, nor does it give her lessons in positive and healthy self-care.

On one hand, a girl in an alcoholic family has a powerful incentive to placate, comfort and nurture her disorderly parents; and on the other, she senses a completely normal and natural desire to have her own emotional and physical needs taken care of. Such a situation is bound to create tremendous inner conflict.

In a healthy and integrated family the conflict might be resolved by allowing the child the opportunity to learn the benefits of both giving and receiving, of thinking of oneself in addition to thinking of others, of selflessness and selfishness.

But in an alcoholic family . . . ?

So what choices does such a girl have? With her limited experience and knowledge, how does she resolve the conflict between having to give and wanting to take?

Too often she solves the problem by avoiding the choice altogether, by denying her desires and deadening her feelings generally. She becomes a giver but the giving is hardly selfless. It is a way of quieting her own unvoiced desires.

Gilda, a 35-year-old psychotherapist told me, "I was a 22-year-old college student before I heard the idea that it was okay for a woman to put her own needs before the needs of other people. I was stunned by the concept! I am not exaggerating when I say that the thought of taking my own needs and desires into consideration when making a decision had simply never entered my head. It was an unheard-of possibility. My mother had always told me to think of other people first. Take care of your brother, watch your sister, what does your father want, how can you make your mother happy? Those were the messages sent me. Never did anyone in my family ever say to me, 'Now, Gilda, what is it that you want?' My entire self-worth was tied up in my providing services to other people. Whenever I dared put myself first, I felt terribly guilty and selfish, like a total failure as a human being, so I'd try to redeem myself by redoubling my efforts to help others. And, quite honestly, it didn't matter a whit to me whether they really needed or wanted my help. I was going to take care of them, by God, because that was the only way I knew how to feel useful and important. I'm sure that's why I became a mental health counselor so I could feel good by taking care of other people."

Gilda's behavior is neither unusual nor unexpected in adult daughters of alcoholics. Here are some more examples:

• Elena was a steady source of information and advice to her many friends with physical or emotional difficulties. If a friend developed a backache, Elena knew of just the right orthopedic surgeon to call. She gave diet books to her overweight friends and the names of marriage counselors to those considering divorce. If counseling didn't work, Elena knew a good lawyer. Meanwhile, Elena herself got fatter and fatter, her marriage faltered and her health deteriorated. Why couldn't she follow her own good advice?

• When Dottie's husband came down with a severe case of the flu, she insisted he go directly to bed and stay there until the doctor gave him permission to go back to work. "Your health is too important to risk," she intoned as she dished out homemade soup. Two weeks later Dottie was doing housework, grocery shopping and crosstown errands with a temperature of 102 degrees.

"Somebody's got to keep the household running," she moaned.

"Besides, it's only the flu." Why was her husband's health more important than her own?

• Myrna could always be counted on in a crunch. If your car broke down and you needed a ride, you could call Myrna. Did you need an extra five place settings of sterling for a big dinner? A place to spend the night? An extra pair of hands to clean out the basement? You could always count on Myrna. And when Myrna was in a car crash that left her with one wrist and a leg in plaster, her friends all pitched in to return the favors she had done them. Why did Myrna politely reject their offers of help? Why did she hire help instead of accepting it from her friends? Why could she give but not take?

Emotional Deadness

An alcoholic family with its denial and deceits kills the honesty, pleasure, vitality, feelings and common-sense of its members. It is a system that values deadening of sensibilities more than the rich, deep feelings and moods that come naturally with true emotional aliveness. Image is esteemed over reality, pride over truth, glory-seeking over honest effort, and control over spontaneity.

Because such an atmosphere provides children with only the most shaky foundation for feelings of self-worth, we end up accepting ourselves almost exclusively in terms of what other people tell us we should be.

For men in our society this usually translates into achievement and success as it is measured by money, status, power and sexual prowess.

For women it means nurturing in the form of kindness, generosity, selflessness and service to others. These values, of course, are not unique to sons or daughters of alcoholics. Ambitious boys and good girls are admired in every strata of our society. And there is certainly nothing intrinsically wrong with these values. In proper proportion both ambition and selflessness are admirable qualities in any person.

Yet I believe that boys and girls growing up in alcoholic families are encouraged, both actively and passively, to take on these traits in a way that is neither admirable nor healthy.

These dominant cultural messages are expanded upon, magnified and exaggerated by family alcoholism. Boys become obsessive glory-seekers, girls become self-effacing doormats. There is no balance.

This imbalance is often disguised by two especially destructive messages alcoholic and co-dependent parents send their children . . .

Keep up a good front at all times because the family pride depends on it.

Don't acknowledge your real feelings because exposing the truth will annihilate you and destroy the family.

In order to live up to these powerful parental dictates, we employ a number of self-destructive strategies —

— We deaden our physical and emotional awareness.

— We withdraw from true intimacy and sharing with those we profess to love.

— We martyr ourselves to the supposed needs of others.

— We are compulsively conformist, yet inwardly defiant.

— And we selfishly impose our will on our loved ones in the name of their own good.

Growing Up

If we are to escape the tyranny of childhood pain, we must grow up in the real world. *And the first lesson of growing up is learning to take care of our own basic needs.*

How can we unselfishly give to others when we are so needy ourselves?

As adults we must practice the every day care of the physical self. This includes healthy eating, good and appropriate exercise, rest, relaxation and stress management. It is important to recognize when we have reached our physical and emotional limits so that we do not deplete ourselves with childish heroics that leave us weakened, exhausted and vulnerable to illness.

And finally we must recognize that as adult children of alcoholics, we face a high risk of developing addictions and co-dependencies.

Adult children of alcoholics are prone to chemical dependency problems. The risk is both hereditary and learned. ADULT CHILDREN WHO DRINK HEAVILY OR WHO USE LEGAL AND ILLEGAL DRUGS FOR RECREATION, RELAXATION OR STRESS REDUCTION WILL DEVELOP THE SAME PROBLEMS THEY HATED IN THEIR PARENTS.

Alcohol, drugs, smoking, compulsive eating, lying and more . . .

Are we shaking an accusatory finger at our parents when more honestly we could be pointing that finger in our own direction? Are we just a bit too eager to be judge, jury and executioner of villains from the past, and a bit too reluctant to take our own inventory here and now? How do we measure up in the self-responsibility department?

Isn't it time we took stock of ourselves in the present and started taking care of ourselves for a change?

11

Avoiding Martyrdom To Self-Neglect

Whether the goal is to produce changes in cognitions, beliefs, feelings, behavior, motivations, etc., there can be no doubt that the therapist's business is the more or less deliberate, self-conscious production of change.

— *Hans H. Strupp, M.D.*

Picture this: In about 1961 one of my alcoholic relatives — let's call him Uncle Herbert — who held an important position with a major national corporation, started having problems on the job because of his drinking. A sympathetic executive officer took Uncle Herbert aside and said something along the lines of, "Good God, man, get a hold on yourself." He then slipped Uncle Herbert a card with the name of a New York psychoanalyst written on it. "Did me a world of good," the executive said cryptically.

Uncle Herbert, who still had his wits about him enough to realize this subtle exchange between him and the boss should be construed as a direct order to shape up, immediately called the shrink for an appointment.

After several months of thrice weekly analytical sessions, the doctor explained to Herbert that his drinking, though troublesome, was not really the problem. It was merely a symptom of a deeper underlying unconscious conflict rooted in childhood. With proper therapy the conflict could be resolved, at which point Herb's alcoholism would subside because the major underlying disorder would be cured.

"Does this mean I don't have to stop drinking now?" Uncle Herbert asked.

The doctor took a firm stand. "When you have made sufficient progress in analysis, you'll no longer need to drink abusively."

Uncle Herbert stayed in analysis for five years, finally dropping out when his company forced him into early retirement with a reduced pension. Did he ever resolve his childhood conflicts and quit drinking? Nope. He died at age 56 of cirrhosis of the liver.

Uncle Herbert received the highest standard of care available to alcoholics at that time. During the 1950's and '60s there were no specialized chemical dependency units, no widely accepted disease concept of addiction, no effective treatment other than Alcoholics Anonymous.

Fortunately times have changed. Today we recognize alcoholism and chemical dependency as primary diseases and the first order of business in recovery is: Get sober and straight.

Co-dependency is also gaining recognition as part and parcel of chemical dependency problems. Again the message is loud and clear: Co-dependents must overcome their denial, acknowledge that their life has become unmanageable and take action to change self-destructive behaviors.

We have learned much in the last 25 years. The enlightened wisdom of today tells us that people can recover from alcoholism and co-dependency. We don't need to resolve all of our inner conflicts before positive change can occur.

Recovery can't wait for us to come to grips with our so-called underlying problems. Chemical dependency and co-dependency are not symptoms.

They are the real thing.

Now, picture this: The year is 1987. It's nine o'clock on a Saturday morning. A woman therapist who specializes in treating depression in adult daughters of alcoholics is addressing a small group of hung-over, overweight, unhappy women. The air is heavy with cigarette smoke.

"You have a right to your depression," the therapist says gently. "You have survived a terrible ordeal and you have a right to your pain."

Several woman nod comprehendingly, others just smoke, eyes downcast.

"I eat when I'm depressed," one woman says, kneading her heavy thighs. "I just get started on food and I can't stop. I feel hungry all the time."

"I can really relate to that," another woman says, and other group members nod their heads in agreement. She adds, "I know I'd feel better if I could just stop eating so much junk."

"I think we've all felt bad and tried to eat our way out of it," says the therapist. "And then when that didn't work, we tried to starve the depression out by eating nothing but parsley and grapefruit. But weight isn't the issue here. Sue's talking about real depression. Right, Sue?"

"Yeah," Sue says.

"How does it feel for you, Sue? Can you share your feelings with the group?"

Sue begins to talk about how she gets really down. The therapist skillfully guides her into talking about her relationships with her parents when she was growing up, her fear and hatred of her alcoholic mother, her ambivalence toward her father and her confusion over her own role in the family. Sue begins to cry as she recalls the lonely lost times, and the therapist and other group members give her a lot of support.

Afterwards Sue feels a sense of relief. Many months later, the group is still dealing with heavy emotions and all the group members have been able to unload the negative feelings of growing up in an alcoholic family. But Sue still feels bad. And she's still eating. And eating. And eating.

But she should feel better, she tells herself. After all, she'd grasped a lot of the dynamics of her family. She now had a fairly good acceptance of the bad feelings that had seemed so unacceptable before.

Finally Sue got the courage to bring up the problem again in group. "I've been wondering if it might help if I could just get my diet under control."

"Diet," said Iris. "I'm for it. The chocaholic's guide to quick weight loss. Sign me up."

"Diet," said another with a trace of bitterness in her voice, "diet is a four-letter word." Everyone laughed. The therapist smiled. "I hear you," she said. "I hear what you're saying. But that's a temporary solution, a quick fix for a much deeper problem. Eating junk is not the real problem. Compulsive eating is merely an ineffective way of coping with the unresolved pain of growing up in a dysfunctional family. It's a superficial manifestation of our real problem. We need to spend much more time working through these emotions, dealing with our pain and sense of loss and guilt. Once we have resolved those issues, dealing with other areas in our life will be much easier . . ."

Wait a minute! What's going on here? Is this *deja vu* or a time warp or what? Isn't that essentially the same message that enabled alcoholics to continue drinking while participating in intensive psychoanalysis 30 years ago? Haven't we all pretty much agreed that chemical dependency and co-dependency are not symptoms, but real problems?

Why would adult children want to use theories and methods that failed with their parents? Haven't we learned anything in the last three decades?

As we have seen, one of the major problems of adult children is that we don't take care of ourselves. This characteristic is not a symptom, not an outward sign of some profound underlying disorder. Self-neglect is a firmly entrenched pattern of behavior. And if we are to recover, we must deal with the problem directly.

We can spend hours and hours in insight therapy groups exploring the past and "coming to terms with" the anxiety monsters in our closets, all the time waiting for the magic time when we will be transformed from ugly, awkward, frightened ducklings into magnificent swans — or fearless eagles boldly soaring where no man has gone before.

Those magic transformations are rare outside of fairy tales. The real truth is more mundane. As one therapist put it, "Therapy is change, not peanut butter."

Integrating Insight and Behavior Change

Insight is a perception into the inner nature or real character of a thing. When we seek insight into the workings of the physical world, we can usually find one true and correct answer to our questions. Why is the sky blue? Why do the tides turn? Why does water boil at 212° Fahrenheit? These questions have answers that anyone, if given the proper knowledge and tools, can decipher.

But when we ask, "Why? Why? Why am I the way that I am?" the answer is frequently, "Because you are." We can dig up family trees, we can try to recall the family determinants . . . but how far back do we go? When do we stop? Some people are now into past life regression therapy. How many of our past lives do we therapize? Which one is the real culprit causing our present problems?

And what about our current life? How reliable is our memory of what happened in childhood? In adolescence? Ten years ago? Last Wednesday? (Research suggests that memory of early childhood, for example, is not very reliable at all, and that memory in general tends to be a hit and miss affair, with imagination filling in many of the blanks.)

And why is it that Jaimie, whose mom and dad were both alcoholic, turned out to be a college president, while Jack, whose parents never drank, ended up on skid row? We are told, "The same fire that melts the butter boils the egg." Small solace, since we have no way of knowing whether we're butter or egg, or even how hot the fire is, if there is one.

So we generally settle for acceptable answers.

In truth, there are no pat answers, no perfect explanations that make the pieces of the personal puzzle fall neatly into place. And there is no revelation, no universal solvent, that will automatically make everything better.

We humans are too complex. We may never discover the true causes or real nature of our deepest, most strongly felt emotions. All we know is that all humans are hardwired to experience intense feelings of love and anger, joy and fear, happiness and grief. It is our nature to feel.

Do we recover by seeking insight into the twists of our inner psyche or do we start changing specific behaviors that are causing us harm in the here and now?

For me, the answer is that we do both.

Insight and Change

- *We can simultaneously do grief work and learn stress management techniques.*
- *We can explore our inner rage while we are learning to modify our eating habits.*
- *We can examine our fear of abandonment while we kick marijuana and stop going one toke over the line.*

In other words . . .

We can gain insight into our emotional weaknesses while we start taking care of our physical selves.

These are especially important points to keep in mind because over the years adult children employ a variety of physically destructive methods in an attempt to eradicate ever-present feelings of anxiety and fear — alcohol and drugs, heavy smoking, over-eating, over-sleeping, workaholism, compulsive talking and arguing, compulsive sexual behavior.

Ironically our compulsive "solutions" to anxiety make our lives worse, not better. These ersatz anxiety-reducers inevitably make life more complicated. They are diversions, not solutions to anxiety. And they are costly diversions: They not only lower the general quality of our lives, but they have an aspect that leads to what has been called "sub-intentional suicide" — a kind of self-destruction by default.

While many adult children try to diminish their pervasive fear by avoiding all risks (and thus most opportunities), some of the most frightened people — male and female — adopt what seems like a don't-give-a-damn attitude. They laugh in the face of fear, taking increasing risks with their health and safety.

These people specialize in walking along the edge of disaster. They scoff at danger and they disdain the margin of safety. The "edgework" specialist seems to court self-destruction. Edgeworkers drink heavily, drive fast, smoke two packs a day and go, go, go.

Sinclair Lewis, a winner of the Nobel Prize for Literature, recognized this behavior in his collaborator, Paul de Kruif. A man of gargantuan appetites and a flamboyant risk-taker, de Kruif revelled in swimming in a bay full of sharks. After listening to his friend brag about swimming out further and further each day in the shark-infested waters, Lewis commented, "You have a will to destruction, Paul."

"You've got me wrong," de Kruif replied. "It is only the determination of a coward to conquer fear of destruction."

Of Cowardice and Courage

Is it the fear of destruction that motivates adult children to abuse our bodies and minds? Is it fear of experiencing the discomfort of real feelings that leads us to medicate ourselves with alcohol, drugs and food? Is it fear of intimacy that turns us into workaholics who have neither the time nor energy to get really close to those we love? Is it fear of failure that makes us all-or-nothing perfectionists who too often do nothing toward making ourselves well? Are we cowards who cling to the past because we are afraid of the present?

To face the present without our chemical crutches, to slow down, to test our discipline, to risk failure . . . all of this takes courage.

Change is frightening.

Yet courage is not the absence of fear. Courage is facing the challenges before us in spite of all the fear. If we accept the challenge of making ourselves healthy, if we take the responsibility for our own well-being, if we fail and try again and again, then slowly, slowly our fears subside.

Accepting the challenge of really taking care of ourselves makes us strong, gives us a certain sense of integrity, makes our minds feel sharp. For the first time we start feeling that life is not just a trial, but an adventure. And slowly, slowly, as we gain mastery and control over our lives, our despair transforms into hope and our cowardice into courage.

12

Somato-Psychics: The Food/Mood Connection

Our daily diet grows odder and odder
It's a wise child who know it's own fodder.

— *Ogden Nash*

Louise, a 29-year-old teacher, went to the doctor complaining of chronic fatigue. She had taken half a dozen sick days in the last few months, not because of any specific illness, but because she simply felt bad. "I feel like I've got a case of chronic mononucleosis. I'm literally dragging myself through the day, and I have trouble sleeping at night. I have weak spells and palpitations. I can't go on like this." Before conducting lab tests, the doctor wisely took a thorough history, quizzing Louise about her eating and exercise habits, whether she was taking any medications or over-the-counter preparations, and whether she was happy with her job and personal life.

It didn't take very long for the physician to spot a suspicious, but all-too-common pattern in Louise's lifestyle. She'd been fighting 15 extra pounds for several years, using a combination of self-discipline and over-the-counter diet pills in an effort to shed the stubborn pounds.

She sometimes succeeded in losing weight . . . temporarily. "In the past five years," she'd confide to friends, "I've lost at least 200 pounds." The problem was, of course, that she always regained the weight. And sometimes a little bit more.

Typically, Louise started the day with a cup of coffee, a 12-hour timed release appetite suppressant, and a multi-vitamin pill. No breakfast. Lunch consisted of a cup of plain yogurt, a piece of fruit, a rice cracker and black coffee. She also drank coffee during her morning and afternoon breaks. Dinner was a well-balanced meal of meat, complex carbohydrates, and fresh vegetables. "I'm very interested in good nutrition," Louise explained.

"That may be true," the doctor told her, "but you're still undernourished and over-medicated. You're going the whole day on about 250 calories and caffeine. You're depleting your body of fuel, and you may have upset your glucose metabolism. The appetite suppressants you're taking contain ingredients which can stimulate the adrenal glands, causing sleeplessness, anxiety, heart palpitations and high blood pressure."

The doctor ran a series of tests, including a glucose tolerance test. The results showed that an otherwise healthy Louise suffered from unstable blood glucose (or blood sugar) levels. Because glucose is the main fuel for the body, Louise would feel weak and shaky when her blood sugar level dropped below normal.

"People who diet frequently and who skip meals often suffer from periods of hypogycemia or low blood sugar," the doctor explained. "This condition can be easily corrected by following a sensible diet."

Louise cringed inwardly. "Sensible diet" sounded a lot like "sensible shoes." No fun at all. Carrot sticks and bran, with a handful of raisins tossed in, along with a lettuce leaf and a stringy stalk of celery. Rabbit food.

The doctor continued, "I want you to throw out your diet pills, start eating breakfast and a more substantial lunch, and a smaller dinner. You're not getting enough calories, protein or carbohydrates during the day."

"But I eat yogurt and fresh fruit," Louise protested. "Those are healthy foods."

"Of course they are," the doctor agreed, "but they are not magic foods. They have no special properties. A cup of yogurt is basically a cup of milk — 8 grams of protein, that's all. The culturing process adds beneficial bacteria, but it doesn't increase the nutritional value of the basic ingredients."

The doctor went on to explain that in order to lead a high-energy life, Louise needed to feed her body the fuel it runs on best — which is high quality protein and complex carbohydrates, not caffeine and vitamin pills. He said, "In effect, you're filling your tank with high octane fuel at night while your engine is idling. But the next day there's nothing left to go on but vapors. You feel tired and weak because you're running on empty."

He also assured her that eating breakfast and lunch would not make her gain weight, as she feared, as long as she didn't fill up on high calorie junk food, too. In fact, recent research shows that people who go all day without eating, then eat a large evening meal, will gain weight. Yet, eating the same amount of food during the day, when we are active, does not make us gain weight. By starving herself during the day, Louise was actually sabotaging her efforts to slim down.

Louise started to follow the doctor's suggestions and she started feeling better within a week. "The hardest part was taking time for breakfast and lunch," she says. "I'm so used to being pushed for time that eating regular meals sometimes seems like a real inconvenience, but I feel so much better, it's worth it."

Adult Children Have Special Nutritional Problems

In today's society a fast paced life seems to be the norm. We always seem to have too much to do and not enough time to do it in. Both men and women are juggling the demands of career and family, child care and commitment to the community. Such responsibilities can foster a lifestyle which saps us of the energy we need to function at an optimum level. When we examine this lifestyle, we see

- Irregular eating habits . . .
- Perpetual dieting . . .
- Inadequate exercise . . .
- Too much coffee, tobacco, alcohol, marijuana, Valium, cocaine . . .
- Too much stress, not enough rest . . .
- And not enough personal time . . .

All of these factors add up — and they don't just add up, they multiply, augment each other and contribute to a chronic energy drain.

These problems of lifestyle seem to be especially acute in adult children of alcoholics. Why is this? I think one of the main reasons is that in alcoholic homes, irregular habits are the norm.

Children of alcoholics don't know how to live a healthy lifestyle because their parents didn't model healthy behavior. Hit and miss meals, emotional and physical exhaustion, and constant stress are normal components of homelife to adult children.

Then there is the heredity factor. We know that alcoholism runs in families. Scandinavian research clearly shows that the propensity for becoming alcoholic is based on biology, not on upbringing or environment. It doesn't matter how terrible a person's home life is — if there is no history of alcoholism in biological relatives, that person has a low risk of becoming alcoholic himself. And if you are raised in the most wonderful foster home imaginable, you still have a higher risk of becoming alcoholic if you have biological parents who are alcoholic.

ADULT CHILDREN OF ALCOHOLICS FACE A HIGH BIOLOGICAL RISK OF DEVELOPING CHEMICAL DEPENDENCY PROBLEMS.

The hereditary factor may affect more than just a predisposition to addiction. After studying hundreds of adult children of alcoholics, we have seen three specific problems over and over again. These problems occur at a much higher rate in adult children than in adults who report no family history of alcoholism.

1. Chemical Dependency (to alcohol, legal and illegal drugs, and tobacco).
2. Blood Sugar Disorders (both adult onset diabetes and reactive hypoglycemia).
3. Chronic Endogenous Depression (a blue mood and sense of hopelessness that continues regardless of external circumstances).

We don't know why adult children seem to have more trouble with these problems. Maybe alcoholism, depression and defects in blood sugar metabolism are somehow related. We don't know and there is no clear-cut scientific evidence to offer us an explanation.

But for our purposes all we need to know is that if you are the child of an alcoholic, you have a higher than average chance of developing blood sugar problems and depression, especially if you drink, skip meals, follow fad diets or are a junk food junkie. You may also be hit harder by the stress and strain of a competitive lifestyle than a person who inherits a less sensitive nervous system and metabolism.

I believe that our moods are irrevocably intertwined with the way we treat our bodies. If we neglect or abuse our physical selves, we are abusing ourselves mentally and emotionally. We may struggle and search and suffer in our quest for emotional well-being and happiness. We may spend thousands of dollars for therapists, retreats, seminars and groups. We may reach out desperately for the help we know we need . . .

Yet here is a basic fact that cannot be ignored: All the counseling, therapy, psychology and insight in the world will not put an end to unpleasant feelings that are caused by a body screaming out for proper care and feeding. Our physical and emotional selves cannot be separated.

We have all heard of psychosomatic illnesses, a phenomenon in which physical problems — real illnesses — are created or made worse by the mind.

I believe that many miserable adult children suffer from somato-psychic illnesses, that is mental and emotional problems intensified or caused by the biochemical interactions of an abused body.

This is an important concept. Without going into an anatomy and physiology lesson, and at the risk of oversimplifying, let me say this: The unstable blood sugar levels self-neglectful adult children are prone to can cause a variety of unpleasant physical and emotional symptoms including depression, weakness, nervousness, anxiety, headaches, sleep problems, mental confusion and despair. And in most cases the kinds of blood sugar problems adult children suffer from can be corrected by changes in lifestyle that emphasize eating well, physical activity and stress reduction.

Stress Reduction

Here are three stress-reducing exercises that can help you learn to reward yourself with the small, ordinary, and free pleasures of life.

Stress-Reduction Exercise 1:

Small Delights   (5 minutes a day)

Adult children are often multi-taskers. That means we do three things at once, with little awareness or pleasure in any of it. This is an exercise of the physical senses. Its purpose is to increase your awareness of the pleasure of an ordinary activity, in this case, drinking a cup of coffee.

STEP 1. Stop and consider this for a moment: You possess five senses — hearing, seeing, touch, taste and smell. As you sit in your kitchen in the morning drinking a cup of coffee, you have it within your power to enjoy that coffee as much or more than anyone else in the world — if you become aware of your senses. Think about it . . . your coffee tastes and smells just as good as the coffee Prince Charles and Princess Diana are drinking right now in Kensington Palace.

STEP 2: Choose a sturdy mug or a delicate china cup, whatever you prefer, but make it special. Hold the full cup between both hands, letting the warmth seep into your fingers. As the fragrant steam rises, inhale the aroma deeply, savoring it. Enjoy the play of light on the liquid's surface, watch the sparkle and shine for a moment. Then slowly sip, relishing the first pungent burst of taste on your tongue. Then drink deeply, allowing the lovely sensations of the moment to fill you with pleasure. For a few moments, think of nothing but the pleasure you are experiencing.

STEP 3: Everyday, as you go through your daily routine, take a few moments to truly use your five senses. Immerse yourself in the sound of a bird singing, or the touch of fabric on your body, or the geometric lines in brickwork. Our senses are rather like our muscles. If we don't exercise them, they atrophy. Exercise your senses for the sheer pleasure of it.

Stress Reduction Exercise 2:

Noticing the World   (5 minutes a day)

One hectic year, I discovered I had been so busy with my work and civic responsibilities that I had completely missed springtime, summer and fall. As I ran from meeting to meeting, from dawn to dusk, the leaves budded, flowers bloomed and withered and died, the leaves turned brown and fell. When I looked up it was winter again. I missed a whole year of seasons, a whole year of my life, without even noticing it had slipped away from me. Has that ever happened to you? I vowed not to let it happen to me again.

That was seven years ago. I devised the following exercise for myself and I have used it everyday since then. It has brought me immeasurable pleasure.

Stand at a window and look outside. Or better yet, stand outside and look around you. Look at the sky, the clouds, the patches of blue and gray. Notice how the clouds move and change. Look at the buildings. Watch how shadow and light play along the surfaces. Move your eyes over the landscape. Pick out textures and colors and shades. Notice them. Look at a tree or a flower or a weed. Has it grown since yesterday. How has it changed? Smell the air. Is it sweet? Polluted? Ripe with street smells? How does it compare to yesterday? Better or worse? How's the temperature? Broiling, freezing, nasty, perfect? How does it compare with yesterday? Does it look like it will be better tomorrow? As each day passes, pay attention to the changes in the sky, the weather, the air, the plants, the trees, the flowers, even the weeds. Watch the seasons unfold. Appreciate the warm days and the foul days, for they are the days in which we live. And just as a winter storm can be followed by a day of clear crisp loveliness, our emotional storms can be followed by emotional clarity and peace. If we will only take the time to notice the changes.

Stress Reduction Exercise 3:

Time Out (1-5 minutes)

Would you like to learn how to relax under pressure? You can actually use the power of your mind to slow your pulse and unknot your muscles. This is an exercise of mental imagery. To experience this most fully, you might want a friend to read the following words to you. Or better yet, tape record the words in your own voice. The words should be read slowly and evenly, with pauses of several seconds between lines. By practicing regularly, you can train your mind to help you cope with stress. Then, whenever you feel the pressure mounting, sit back, close your eyes for a minute or two, and relax.

Just sit back and make yourself comfortable. Allow your eyes to close . . .

As you listen to my voice, you will feel a growing sense of relaxation and comfort in your body . . .

We are going to count from one to five and as we do . . .
You will imagine yourself feeling a deep sense of peace and
tranquility . . .
    one . . .
    Just beginning . . .
    letting relaxation spread through your scalp . . .
    and your face . . .
    and your neck . . .
    two . . .
    going down deeper . . .
    more relaxed . . .
    into your shoulders . . .
    and arms . . .
    and hands . . .
    three . . .
    breathing easy . . .
    every breath taking you deeper . . .
    into peace and tranquility and calm . . .
    Feel the relaxation in your chest . . .
    in your belly . . .
    and down . . .
    deeper into relaxation . . .
    four . . .
    Feel the relaxation in your stomach . . .
    and hips . . .
    and legs . . .
    and feet . . .
    down deeper into complete tranquility . . .
    Totally calm . . .
    deeply relaxed . . .
    almost there . . .
    five . . .
    Tranquil, calm, peaceful . . .
    Let yourself drift with these lovely feelings . . .
    Feeling so calm . . .
    and when you are ready . . .
    just open your eyes . . .
    all the way up . . .
    back to alertness . . .
    bringing these calm feelings with you . . .
    totally refreshed.

Active Relaxation

Not all relaxation is passive, slow, or restful. Sometimes we need to work our bodies in order to relax. For example, when I am writing, I may sit for hours and hours without moving anything but my fingers and eyes as I work at a computer. At the end of the day, I need to relax with a fast paced walk around the neighborhood, a hike in the woods, or a swim in the river. The last thing I need, no matter how tired I am, is to collapse on the sofa.

On the other hand, when I teach a class or seminar I am very active both physically and emotionally. I'm on my feet, moving around the room and engaged in intense interaction with the seminar participants. When it's over, I'm beat, totally drained. I need rest, peace, quiet, a time to reflect and recharge my batteries.

The point is this: Recreational activities which are relaxing for one person at a particular time can be draining to a different person or at another time.

We need to balance what we do for relaxation with what we do for work. If our job is sedentary, hum-drum, undemanding, or boring, we are wise to spend our free time in active and exciting pursuits.

If our work keeps us running physically and emotionally, if it's fast paced and thrilling, we need some time to recoup our energies. We need rest.

Failure to recognize these separate needs can cause severe problems for couples who work at jobs that have a different level of demandingness, but who spend their leisure time together. The results can be disastrous unless compromises are made.

What we all need is balance. Enough sleep, enough activity, a little excitement, and some moments of tranquility. We need to manage our lives wisely. Taking care of ourselves doesn't mean an end to self-indulgence and pleasure. It means managing our lives so that we can get the most pleasure possible . . . with the fewest negative consequences. So have fun, eat an ice cream cone, stay out late, sleep in if you want to.

But not every day.

Patterns of Care-Less Eating

Over the years I've observed a certain pattern of eating that is common among adult children who suffer from moodiness, fatigue, lack of vitality and excess weight. It's a pattern of eating that's virtually guaranteed to produce somato-psychic symptoms.

Does this sound familiar?

• No breakfast or a breakfast high in sugar or caffeine.

• Skipped meals.

• Light eating during the day; heavy eating during the evening.

• Nighttime snacking to assuage gnawing hunger.

• Lots: Sugar, junk food, salt, fat, tobacco, caffeine, simple carbohydrates.

• Little: Fresh fruits and vegetables, whole grains.

These erratic eating habits are frequently accompanied by sporadic bursts of dietary self-discipline that are meant to slim us down or perk us up. Unfortunately, these attempts are usually short-lived and sometimes counter-productive as in the case of fad diets and magic-bullet, one-shot cures.

Lose 14 Pounds in One Week With Hypnobese!

Try the All-Buffalo Quick-Weight-Loss Diet

Lose Up To 50 Pounds Without Dieting!
Cal-Ban 3000 Tablets

Firm Up Flabby Thighs In One Week
Sexercise Yourself!

Lose 25 Pounds In 14 Days
Rice Diet

Natural Energizers — Okra-Pick-Me-Up Pills
(They're Super-Charged!)

Tap Your Hidden Power Reservoir With
CellulosePLUS
(Cedar Shavings With Added Vitamins)

These come-ons promise an effortless quick-fix to problems that have been a long time in the making. Primed by technologies that give us instant light, color, sound and motion, as well as one-stop shopping and effortless transportation, we tend to gravitate toward the quick-fix, toward the effortless solution to complex personal problems.

Of course, one-stop effortless solutions exist for every social and psychological ill: such solutions, however, turn out to be simple, painless and wrong.

All of us are looking for a quick-fix, a sure-fire, painless technique of recovery. No such thing exists. When we launch ourselves into periodic bouts of Spartan self-discipline, which usually means drastic diets and rigorous exercise for a period of a week or two, we are doing ourselves no favors. Such a regimen more often than not turns out to be an energy drainer. Any positive effects are short-lived and transitory. And in the long run we end up feeling like failures.

Fatigued, unhappy or overweight adult children don't need another diet. We need a new lifestyle.

Avoiding the
All Or Nothing Pitfall

Remember, you are a troubled person taking on a most difficult task — the taming of a turbulent past and all the bad habits that come from a lifetime of denial, fear and self-neglect.

Give yourself a break. All the breaks you can.

Desperate adult children have a tendency to sabotage themselves with an all-or-nothing approach to self-improvement. We make Great Resolutions with High Expectations.

The scenario goes something like this: "Okay, I'm really going to get my act together. I'm going to improve everything. Natural food only and an hour of aerobics everyday.

Instead of pigging-out, I'm going to meditate every night. No more screwing around. I'm changing all the way this time."

Don't do it.

You will fail and your failure may make you feel depressed and miserable. We don't have to become paragons of virtue. We don't need to be perfect, not in 14 days anyway. It's important to set achievable goals, not impossible ones.

Repeat: You don't need to be perfect.

A lot of small changes can add up to a big improvement. And that's good.

13

Chemical Independence

*Everybody who tells you how
to act has whisky on their breath.*

— John Updike

A significant number of adult children begin to deal with the unresolved issues of their family alcoholism after developing chemical dependency problems of their own. Usually these are men and women who get into treatment early — in their 20s or 30s. They get sober and straight, they go to their meetings, but still . . . something is lacking. Then they discover an unsettling fact: While they may be recovering from chemical dependency, they are still unrecovered from the co-dependency problems they developed while growing up in an alcoholic family.

And the same things that keep them sober — the programs, the steps, the living one day at a time and saying the serenity prayer until their tongues grow numb — these strategies that worked so well in their recovery from chemical dependency may have limited value in the recovery from co-dependency.

Still, these adult children — the ones who are sober and straight — are one jump ahead of the game. They are free to continue on their journey to self-realization, drug free, unencumbered with the self-stultifying health drainers of chemical dependency.

What about the rest of us? Does everyone seeking self-realization have to go on the wagon and become adamant and self-righteous teetotalers? Is it possible to find love and happiness and still have a Bloody Mary or a Bud Lite now and then? Can we go one toke over the line on Saturday night and have self-fulfillment the other six days of the week?

Usually this kind of questioning is phrased in a mocking, sarcastic way, because we live in a culture that promotes the widespread use of drugs — drugs for ills, drugs for pains, and drugs for recreational use, for altering moods, quelling anxieties, for sleep. We are a nation of drug users.

Given that drugs and drug use are so prevalent in our society, let's take a closer look at the implications of drug use for adult children.

One point of vital importance for all adult children to understand is this:

The inability to safely tolerate alcohol and other psycho-active chemicals is an inherited, biological characteristic.

Let's say it another way: The tendency to develop alcohol and drug addiction runs in families. The probability of developing a problem with chemicals increases with

(A) the number of close relatives who have had similar problems.

(B) the biological closeness of the relationship of those who have had chemical problems.

(C) the number and intensity of those problems in one's relatives.

To take this out of the abstract realm of probability and really hammer the point home, let's say: If either one of your biological parents suffered from alcoholism or drug addiction, the chances are that you, too, will become an alcoholic or drug addict if you use alcohol or drugs on a regular basis.

What does this mean in real terms?

1. You can consider yourself a heavy drinker in risk of developing alcohol problems if . . .

- You drink more than two drinks a day.
- You regularly drink six or more drinks at any given time. For example, you don't drink during the week, but you drink heavily on weekends.
- You don't drink on a regular basis, but when you do drink, you get drunk.
- You drink to relieve emotional tension, anger, boredom or insomnia.

You already have a drinking problem if you have suffered from black-outs (you don't remember things that happened while you were drinking), or you are sneaking and lying about how much you drink, or you need to drink to get through the day, or you have had job or legal problems (DWI arrests or other alcohol-related offenses) because of your drinking, or your family and friends are complaining about your drinking.

You don't need to have all of these problems to be an alcoholic, although if you keep drinking, you probably will. In fact, it's important to note at this point that you don't have to be an alcoholic to have a problem with alcohol. You don't have to be an addict or a mainliner or a coke fiend to have a problem with drugs.

Listen: You are probably saying to yourself, "If I ever got as bad as my dad (or mom) was, I'd quit drinking right away. But I'm not that bad yet."

How bad do you have to get? Is there a magic moment when you will sit up and exclaim. "Gosh, I guess I'm finally that bad."

Don't wait until you are as bad as your parent. Ask yourself honestly, "Do I really need drugs in my life? Do drugs really make things better, or is that just an illusion?"

If you do decide to become alcohol and drug-free, you may find that it's harder than you thought. Get help if you need it. You don't have to check into a hospital for a month. Many major treatment centers now provide out-patient counseling. Or call Alcoholics Anonymous. Don't let the disease of alcoholism destroy another generation of your family.

2. You can consider yourself chemically dependent if you smoke marijuana on a regular basis.

The horror of watching a parent destroyed by alcohol is enough to turn some people totally against drinking. Unfortunately, it is not uncommon to find an adult child who spurns liquor, but who smokes marijuana on a regular basis.

For example, Dinah wouldn't touch a drop of alcohol. Both her parents were drunks. While in her teens and early twenties, Dinah had tried drinking, but she hated the way it made her feel. She threw up. She made a fool of herself. She had terrible hang-overs. That was enough to make her swear off completely because she didn't want to end up like her parents.

During her senior year in college, Dinah started smoking marijuana with her boyfriend. She liked it. She liked the dreamy floaty feeling. She liked the way it made her feel protected against the hard-edges of life. And she also liked the fact that she could keep functioning after smoking. Marijuana seemed like a light and harmless high compared to what alcohol did to her. Over the next few years Dinah smoked a little marijuana almost every day. During that time she never felt like she had a problem.

But she did.

Let's not get into an argument about the relative merits of marijuana versus alcohol. That will get us nowhere. Yes, yes, we're all agreed. Alcohol is a drug.

So is marijuana. It is not a neutral herb. If it was, we wouldn't use it to get high.

While marijuana intoxication is not as sloppy and apparent as drunkenness, it does cause a change in feeling, thinking and judgment. I have seen these particular problems in my clients who regularly use marijuana.

• *Emotional flatness.* This may be one of the effects adult children seek. My marijuana-using clients don't feel and react to their surroundings in an appropriate fashion. They seem to be reacting more to internal cues. This emotional flatness damages relationships by hindering the development of intimacy. In short, marijuana users may be present in a relationship but they are not emotionally available.

• *Inability to tolerate even small levels of frustration.* I don't know how marijuana causes this effect but I have seen it many times. It is the opposite of the emotional flatness of intoxication. While stoned, the user under-reacts to his or her environment. When not stoned, there is an over-reaction. Small annoyances flare into disasters. If the lid won't come off the jar of spaghetti sauce, the jar might be shattered against the wall. The door won't open? — smash your fist through it. The ashtray is a few inches out of reach? — kick over the table.

The combination of emotional flatness and emotional over-reaction are especially damaging to children growing up with a stoned parent. I predict that in the next generation we will have a movement called Adult Children of Potheads.

• *Paranoia.* In the 1960s we used to think that it was the harsh laws governing marijuana use that made pot smokers paranoid, not the drug itself. Now the thinking is different.

Smoking marijuana doesn't make people paranoid in the classic sense. It won't make you think the Commies are frying your brain with microwaves unless that happens to be something you normally worry about. What happens is something more like this:

Each of us possesses certain secret fears, worries and concerns. For example, Karen carried inside her deep fears of abandonment that could be traced back to the early death of her beloved father. The fear was always there, hidden, simmering below the surface of her consciousness. Smoking marijuana brought this fear to the forefront, but not in a healthy way. It surged up like a nameless black fog from the sewers of her soul. Karen thought smoking marijuana helped ward off the fog. But it wasn't until she got straight that she was finally able to face her fear and release herself from its bonds. Many of our most basic fears are unnamed and unvoiced, yet they bubble under the layers of our consciousness. This is true for all of us. Yet my marijuana-using clients seem to suffer more from nameless anxiety than do my other clients.

It has been argued that these feelings and behaviors are the result of a personality disorder for which the victim uses marijuana as self-medication. I disagree. I believe emotional flatness, the inability to tolerate frustration and increased nameless anxiety are direct drug effects. Why do I believe this? Because I have seen these symptoms lessen and even disappear within a year after a client stops using.

How do you figure out how much marijuana is too much? What is social smoking and what is chemical dependency?

- If you smoke about once a week, you are at risk of developing a problem.
- If you smoke two or three times a week, you do have a problem.
- If you smoke almost everyday, you are in serious trouble.

If you suffer from any of the same kinds of problems we discussed concerning alcohol use, regardless of how much or how often you smoke, you have a problem. Help for marijuana abuse is available from the same sources that assist people with alcohol problems. Please, if you recognize yourself in these words, seek help immediately. You can improve your life.

3. You can become chemically dependent by using legally prescribed pain medication, sleeping pills or tranquilizers . . . even if you take the drugs according to your doctor's instructions.

We discussed this issue in Chapter 10 when we addressed using medication to treat anxiety. We also risk getting hooked on prescription medication if we suffer from chronic pain, such as backaches, headaches or arthritis.

Lucille, a 55-year-old housewife and mother, had seen her father and brothers die of alcoholism. She didn't drink and she successfully urged her children to stay away from alcohol and illegal drugs. She also volunteered her time to provide drug education in the local schools and she became a highly respected expert on how to develop a grass-roots anti-drug campaign.

Lucille never dreamed she could become a drug addict. But that's exactly what happened. How? She slipped a disc in her back. The pain was excruciating. Her doctor prescribed pain killers and tranquilizers. The pain continued and after a while Lucille had to take twice as many pills to get relief.

Eventually, she had surgery. After a period of convalescence, her doctor took her off all medication.

"You won't need pain pills anymore," he told her. And Lucille agreed. After all, she believed in a drug-free life.

But within two days, she felt awful. Her skin crawled, she felt shaky and irritable. She wanted a pill. But she was too embarrassed to ask her regular doctor. So she called her gynecologist and asked for codeine. She told him an old condition was acting up again. Unsuspicious, he called the pharmacy with the prescription without insisting Lucille come in for an examination. Lucille promised to wean herself off the drugs but whenever she tried she felt awful. Within six months this respectable housewife was getting pills from four different doctors and four different pharmacies. She was a junkie. It wasn't until her family confronted her that she was finally able to get off the pills with medical supervision.

The point is this: If addiction can happen to someone like Lucille, it can happen to anyone. Including you and me. Here are some warning signs:

• Have you taken prescription pain medication, sleeping pills or tranquilizers on a daily basis for more than two weeks?

• Do the pills seem to work less effectively than they used to against your pain?

• Have you tried to cut down or stop taking the pills, but you felt so awful and nervous that you took one and it relieved your nervous feelings?

• Are you hiding the fact that you are taking a lot of pills from your family? Are you getting pills from several different doctors and drug stores?

If you answered yes to two or more of these questions, it's time for a frank discussion with your doctor. You may need medical help to get off the drugs (stopping cold turkey without your doctor's assistance can be dangerous). If you've been using prescription painkillers and relaxers for a long time, you may need special treatment. Please, talk to your doctor today.

4. You can consider yourself chemically dependent if you use tobacco.

By now the addictive nature of tobacco is almost universally acknowledged. (Almost, I say, because the tobacco industry contends that smoking is a harmless pastime and people choose to smoke because they enjoy it.) The surgeon general, the AMA, virtually all health associations and insurance companies recognize the hazards of smoking.

The addiction to nicotine is a health drainer in every sense of the word. It depletes the body of essential vitamins. It weakens the immune system. It increases the likelihood of heart disease, emphysema and other respiratory ailments, cancers of the lungs, throat and mouth. Cigarette smokers report more use of sick leave and other health benefits than non-smokers, which is a major reason why Fortune 500 corporations have started no-smoking policies for employees.

On a more mundane level, most people who smoke develop an insensitivity to odor. Thus, they have no appreciation of the fact that they leave a miasma of stale cigarette smoke behind them wherever they go. Because their taste buds have been charred, they have little appreciation of food unless it is heavily salted.

What are the payoffs from stop-smoking efforts?

- Increased libido
- Greater awareness and pleasure in food
- An enhanced awareness of your living environment
- Fewer chronic heart and respiratory problems
- Greater longevity at a higher quality of life
- Become exemplars of drug-free behavior for children

This last point is often overlooked by adult children who have themselves been raised on the "Don't do as I do, do as I say" rule.

I want to go out on a limb and say: You can't tame your turbulent past unless you become drug free — including cigarettes. Drugs are a self-indulgence, not a self-enhancer. Smokers are inconsiderate of others and abusive toward themselves — whether they know it or not.

The expert who stands behind a podium and mouths high-sounding truths about self-fulfillment and self-worth, and then sneaks off for a cigarette when the public presentation is done is engaging in a parody of self-fulfillment.

And there's an irony in the fact that nurses are schooled in caring for others but have the highest rates of smoking among the professions.

Other ironies abound:

• The parents who become frenzied about a child's experimental use of marijuana, but who smoke and drink with nonchalance.

• The smoker who buys Topol to get the cigarette stains off his teeth, but who remains oblivious to the stains on his lungs.

• Alcohol and drug treatment programs that help their patients recover from the life-threatening addictions of alcohol and other drugs, but who approve of their patients remaining addicted to the life-threatening drug of nicotine.

• The counselor who pontificates on the value of a drug-free life while puffing on a pipe.

Drugs may sometimes make us seem to be more alert and competent, but this always — always — turns out to be an illusion. You are not a better person when on drugs — you are a drug-affected person.

On any journey it's important to remain alert and responsive. And on the journey to self-fulfillment, to self-realization it's especially important to be drug-free, alert and responsive. You cannot tame your turbulent past by soothing or medicating memories and emotions with drugs.

While being drug-free does not automatically bring about instant recovery, a drug-free life is indispensable to growth and a necessary step in taming your turbulent past.

14

Paradox 4: Self-Esteem — Everything-or-Nothing Syndrome

It is of prime importance to recognize that just about everything we've been taught to expect as "normal" in our lives is the stuff of fairy tales and unrealistic dreams.

— *Theodore Isaac Rubin, M.D.*

I know dozens of perfectly decent, bright, moral, caring, productive, creative and attractive men and women who have come out of alcoholic homes and into the world believing: "There is something terribly wrong with me. I am not like other people. I am not normal."

From time to time, everyone questions his "normality", everyone feels alienated from others. At one time or another we all have felt — even if momentarily — like strangers in a strange land.

But those who have studied adult children of alcoholics say that feelings of intense alienation pervade the lives of adult children. One of the lasting legacies of growing up in an alcoholic family appears to be a dim sense of what "normal" is. Because life in an alcoholic home is filled with denial, pretense and confusion, children end up having to guess at how "normal" people act.

And often they guess wrong.

This makes self-esteem a special problem for adult children. When self-esteem is founded on unrealistic notions of what constitutes normal and acceptable behavior, it becomes extraordinarily susceptible to both external and internal threats.

Eddie, a 32-year-old lawyer whose lawyer father was an alcoholic, is a prime example of an adult child who imposes a tremendous pressure on his self-esteem. He truly believes the only way he can be worthy is by being the best at everything he does.

"If I can't excel in an activity," Eddie told me, "I don't want to do it. I want to top the top, be the best that ever was. I think anyone who aims lower than the very top deserves to fail. It's only normal to want to win."

Like many other adult children, Eddie wants to be brave, strong, confident and successful. He wants to be admired and respected. Certainly, there is nothing wrong with having such desires.

Yet for Eddie and many other adult children, the desire to excel is at the very root of self-hate and despair. Why? Because the perfectionistic, "Either/Or" dynamics in alcoholic families leave no room for tolerance, for balance, for acceptance of human limitations.

Children are trained in a thousand subtle ways: Either you are good, or you are bad. Either you are the best, or you are nothing. Either you are the top dog, or you're a son-of-a-bitch. So, what happens is this — The adult child makes a mistake and says, "I am a failure."

If he needs help, he thinks, "I am a weakling."

If she feels fear, she says, "I am a coward."

If she encounters obstacles on the path to success, she believes, "I'll never get what I want."

Or the adult child may set up impossible obstacles for success. "If I can't be at the top, I don't want to be anything." One adult child sneered at a master's degree in psychology because the Ph.D. was the only worthy attainment. He failed to complete a dissertation, dropped out of the Ph.D. program and ended up with no advanced degree at all.

Underlying these attitudes is the belief that "normal" people — the people worthy of esteem — don't have to struggle to get what they want, and they don't make mistakes or ask for help or feel fear.

An adult child mired in self-hate doesn't realize that courage doesn't mean the absence of fear. Courage is going into the unknown in spite of sometimes overwhelming fear.

Brave people often quake in their boots.
Confident people struggle with self-doubt.
Strong, resolute people sometimes falter, break down.
Successful people make mistakes. (Many would argue that you can't be a success without making mistakes — and learning from them.)

Strong, confident, brave, successful people are just as awkward, self-doubting and vulnerable as the rest of us. They spill coffee down their shirt fronts and argue with their mothers and feel nervous in front of an audience. They lose their patience and worry about the wrinkles growing around their eyes and wonder if there might be something odd about their sex drive. This is reality. This is what normal is all about.

Yet being subject to "normal" human blunders, gaffes and limitations is unacceptable to the adult child who believes that striving for excellence is nothing less than striving for perfection. Rather than being founded on realistic assets and achievements, too often an adult child's self-esteem is based on unattainable goals.

I asked a number of adult children who honestly admitted they suffered from low self-esteem to tell me what they thought it would take for them to start feeling better about themselves. Here are some of the responses —

"I'm going to keep searching and struggling until I discover the final answers to my questions. I know there is an ultimate plan and once I find it, then I'll be happy."

— Linda, age 28

"What I need is greater career recognition. I'm not as far along as I should be at this point. I'm making fairly decent money, but I thought I'd have a judgeship by now."

— Tyler, a lawyer, age 39

"If I had my own home — not an apartment, but a real house with a garden and my own furniture, decorated just right with antiques, that would make me feel more equal to my friends."

— Diane, age 41

"My problem is that my parents are against me and so is my husband's mother. They always criticize me and try to get me to do things their way. If I could just get them to accept me, I know I'd like myself better."

— Kimberly, age 22

"I feel as though I'm trudging though a long tunnel of trouble toward a glowing light at the other end. If I can just get to that light I know I will come out of the end of the tunnel a transcendent person. I'm going to be whole and happy and I'll have a hell of a lot to offer the world."

— Quentin, age 33

"What would it take to make me feel good about myself? That's easy! I need to lose 50 pounds, and get a nose job, and my boyfriend could stop chasing around the bars!"

— Trixie, age 24

A consistent theme runs through these very different responses. One woman hopes for ultimate knowledge, another for a nose job. A lawyer wants an appointment to the bench and an apartment dweller wants a house. Very different dreams indeed. Yet, every one of these unhappy adult children is searching for an external solution to a problem of inner unrest.

For these adult children, self-acceptance is predicated almost exclusively in terms of achievement and success as measured by position, status, money, power, approval by others, or physical beauty. Even Linda and Quentin, who seem to be seeking more spiritual goals, are really locked into a struggle for achievement. For what can be a greater achievement than unlocking the ultimate plan of the universe or transcending the troubles of ordinary mortals.

Self-esteem is our own evaluation of how we compare in worth to other people. Do we have as much as they do? Are we smarter? Better looking? Funnier? Stronger? Sexier? Faster? Meaner? Dumber?

Now, you've probably been told that it's not healthy to compare yourself to other people. And, ideally, that's true. But, being human, we just can't help ourselves. We are social creatures and it's quite natural for us to make comparisons between ourselves and our neighbors.

If we find we compare favorably, then we are disposed to think highly of ourselves. We feel that we are worthy.

If we find ourselves to be abnormal or lacking in some way, then we tend to form a low opinion of ourselves. We feel that we are unworthy.

But what if our comparisons don't have any objective basis in reality? What happens to our self-image when our concept of normal or acceptable performance is based on fairy tales and unrealistic dreams? How can our real self ever measure up to the wonderful fantasy self we imagine we should be?

What Is A Self?

We forge our personal identity — our self — from the raw materials provided us in our early years. As nursery rhymes lull us to sleep, they tell us that little boys are made of snakes and snails and puppy-dog tails, while little girls are made of sugar and spice and everything nice. These are cute ways of interpreting the development of self, but the reality is much more complicated and not always cute.

Our values, our beliefs, our traditions, our histories . . . these are the snakes and snails and sacred unicorn horns that

spark the strange alchemy of self-esteem. We are embroiled
in a network of influences that includes heredity, learning,
circumstance and chance. Somewhere in the midst of a
complex chain of interactions, a self-concept forms, a notion
of who we are, tightly interwoven with a *weltanshauung* — a
world-view, a notion of how the world works.

What is a self? Who are we really? Self, said psychologist
William James many years ago, is a social concept, and we
have as many selves as there are groups of people about
whose opinions we care.

Was Robert Frost talking about the glimmers of self in an
insect, when he saw it pause on a page of paper: "I have a
mind myself," wrote Frost, "and I recognize Mind when I
meet with it in any guise."

We encounter other selves in many guises, and these other
selves provide the social milieu, the rich broth, wherein our
own self finds nourishment. And for most of us the family
provides that growth-promoting context, that nourishment.

But families can also be growth-stunting. As Jane Howard
put it in her book *Families*: "Nothing is or ever was more
wonderful, more dreadful or more inescapable than families,
nor are there many words more perplexing to define."

Think back to your early years in your family. Close your
eyes and let your mind roam for a moment. What do you
remember? What were the dominant messages in your
family? What lessons on life do you remember most?

What are the raw materials from which you are forging
your identity? What are the family rules and role models
that influenced and guided your learning and development?

This question is much more difficult to answer than it
seems. We have a natural tendency to protect and defend
ourselves against pain. And when we start dissecting our
roots, we sometimes feel as if we are cutting into our own
flesh with a thin sharp blade.

It may require some extra courage to delve into the morass
of family memories, but it can be an important undertaking,
especially when inquiry proceeds not as an exercise in
brooding and blame, but as a means to understand the
sources of pain and dissatisfaction, and to discover ways to
change, ways of disentangling from the family roots that
bind, constrict and strangle growth.

It's fashionable these days to call the family a "dynamic system". There are all kinds of dynamic systems, from schools of fish to herds of buffalo. Our planetary system is a dynamic system, and as the planets speed through our part of the Milky Way, they are held in formation by the sun's gravity. A dynamic system, in short, is an aggregation of members that exert an influence on each other.

A family is a dynamic system of two or more individuals, where members influence each other in many ways, physically, emotionally, intellectually and spiritually. Family systems do not exert influence through some kind of cold, impartial mathematically precise Newtonian gravitation. The binding elements of family systems consist of security, touch, love, warmth, stimulation, caring and feeding — a constellation of critical factors that make up the human gravity of emotional bonding, attachment.

The early childhood years are a time, says Selma Fraiberg, "when a baby and his parents make their first enduring human partnerships, when love, trust, joy and self-evaluation emerge through the nurturing love of human partners." Of course, there are other elements of this partnership. Babies and young children influence parents and caretakers through smiling and crying and temper tantrums, among other things. And in general older family members influence the younger to accept certain values, beliefs and traditions as good and right and normal.

As a result we look at ourselves and at the world through a many-layered filter of family dogma, ritual, faith and experience. We integrate these family rules into our own personality and code of conduct. This is a normal and natural process. We cannot escape it. The rules we learn in our family may be bewildering, contradictory, or harsh. Regardless of whether we chose to accept them or defy them, we are stuck with them. They become an integral part of our identity.

The alcoholic family is not only a dynamic system, it is as much an educational system as any school with all its accouterments and paraphernalia of learning. And many of life's most important lessons are learned not in the formal schoolroom, under the tutelage and guidance of teachers, principals and aides — *the lasting formative lessons of life are learned in the family system.*

The lessons start at birth and continue, in one way or another, throughout life. Consider this: A child reaches for a toy, pauses in mid-reach and checks out mom or dad, as if to say, "Okay? I'm going after the rubber ducky." Or, more slyly: "Hey, I'm takin' over this place, okay?" Or: "I want that — how about a little help!"

In truly attentive families much of this shorthand communication gets picked up and accurately translated. In the alcoholic family something quite different happens. The child's playfulness may be resented as an intrusion or nuisance. The parent may misread the child's needs or misplace them with her own, giving us warped and inaccurate feedback so that eventually we come to mistrust the truth of what we do and feel.

The thought crops up: "Something is wrong, dreadfully wrong. I am not in tune with my own family." We feel out of kilter . . . repudiated and assaulted. The School of the Family has taught the child not to trust his own feelings and judgments. The chipping away of self-esteem has begun.

Learning Life's Lessons In the School of Dread

For many adult children, the family is *P.S. Dread*. P.S. Dread can be best described as an informal pedagogical system promoting denial, lies, promises, selfish martyrdom, grandiose fantasies, despair and shame.

Oh, love is in there, too. Lots of it. But love gets so mixed up with fear and anger and pride that sometimes we can't tell it apart from a sick kind of emotional dependence and the internal family struggle for control and power. We don't know exactly where we belong nor if we are truly loved.

We learn more than anything that love is capricious, that human attachment is uncertain and sometimes perilous. We learn to hoard love, store it up for the hard times ahead. Love is surely not something to squander.

We don't feel safe in P.S. Dread. We don't feel safe in our families.

Perhaps it was P.S. Dread that poet Alexander Pope had in mind when he wrote, "A family is but too often a commonwealth of malignants". Perhaps it was P.S. Dread that prompted Andre Gide to utter the savage curse: "Families, I hate you!"

And perhaps it was P.S. Dread that anthropologist Ashley Montague had in mind when he called the family "an institution for the systematic production of physical and mental illness in the members".

In her seminal work, *Neurosis and Human Growth*, psychiatrist Karen Horney wrote vividly about the predicament of adults whose self-esteem is warped in a troubled family. Horney believed that neurosis develops when a person's striving for self-realization is thwarted by adverse circumstances.

And what circumstances can be more adverse for a child than the chaos and turbulence of alcoholic and co-dependent parents?

To cope with natural feelings of isolation and helplessness, the child develops strategies for minimizing anxiety, strategies which invariably lead to a growing sense of alienation from self. These include neurotic pride, denial and reinterpretation of events, vindictive scheming against those who have caused pain, avoidance of risky situations or procrastination.

The thwarted individual more or less sacrifices the goal of self-realization in favor of the goal of reducing anxiety, of finding safety and security.

We become stuck.

Horney theorized, "Not only is his real self prevented from a straight growth, but in addition his need to evolve artificial strategic ways to cope with others has forced him to override his genuine feelings, wishes and thoughts."

Dr. Horney could have been speaking directly to an adult child when she said the confused individual ends up not knowing "where he stands or 'who' he is."

But we need some sort of identity. We need a concept of who and what we are. So, because we need a self-image, we manufacture one — and idealized image which promises fulfillment and a sense of worth. We come to expect perfection from ourselves and from others. We not only expect it, we demand it. "In this process," Horney wrote, "he endows himself with unlimited powers and with exalted faculties; he becomes a hero, a genius, a supreme lover, a saint, a god."

This need for perfection, our striving for an idealized self, becomes what Horney calls a "search for glory".

The search for glory corresponds to an inflexibly high and grandiose evaluation of how we are and should be. It is the notion that we are and should be better than other people, that we are above hum-drum existence and that other people should recognize our superiority. We deserve to get everything we want and anything short of this is totally and completely unfair.

An adult child's glory seeking is often invisible. In fact, many adult children appear to be remarkably modest and self-effacing. Yet the inner state of mind is aimed at preserving an inflexible self-image of a powerful, totally in-control person. This rigid stance is based on fear and despair, for the glaring discrepancy between objective reality and our idealized self-image of perfection is so great that even minor disappointments can plunge us into the zero level of depression and self-hate.

The Crash From Glory To Zero

Nowhere is the paradoxical nature of the adult child's personality more evident than in the area of self-esteem. A large portion of the unhappiness and personal conflict adult children experience is caused by the see-saw of self-esteem between the grandiosity of Glory Seeking and the despair of the Zero Level. There is a direct cause-and-effect relationship between the adult child's feelings of self-loathing and the desire to be superior to everyone else.

When we fail to live up to our impossibly high expectations of how we should be, our self-esteem drops to zero level. We are at rock bottom, psychologically frozen.

An adult child at zero level absolutely believes himself to be a creature of total worthlessness. Not only do we believe ourselves to be nothing, but we are convinced that everyone else can look at us and see our worthlessness. Furthermore we believe our situation is totally hopeless. We are nothing, everyone knows it, and we will remain this way forever.

As a therapist I have been privy to the most secret inner thoughts, hopes and fears of numerous men and women who quite literally despise themselves and the lives they are living. They feel like shadow people living unreal and disjointed lives. They feel overwhelmed and numb.

More than anything else, these people tell me they want to feel good. They want to feel better about themselves. They want to be happy. They want me to help them find the key to positive self-esteem.

I used to think I could help raise a client's self-esteem with my displays of unconditional positive regard. I would give them the love and consistent approval they never received as children. I would reinforce their strong points, their accomplishments, their achievements — all of the things about themselves for which they could be proud. Gently, through a gradual process of natural growth, their true inner worth would unfold, slowly and inexorably, like the slow blossoming of a daffodil, petal by petal, culminating in a full fragrant spring flower.

Working together, we would explore the many facets of self and they would by this natural developmental recapitulation reach the unmistakable conclusion that they were indeed worthy people. And we would all live happily ever after.

Just like the Waltons.

Meanwhile, back in the real world . . .

About ten years ago I began to realize that objective positive feedback has little or no lasting impact on a person wallowing at zero level. Simply put this means that if you truly believe you are a worthless person, all my telling you that you are a good and valuable person will do is make you think that I'm a bad judge of character.

So, I'm not going to try to raise your self-esteem by telling you what a good person you are. I'm not going to ask you to look at your good points and all the things you do right.

Because it's not your good points that fill you with self-loathing. You hate yourself when you feel you can't do anything right. You want to be admired and loved, but problems keep getting in the way. You feel like you don't measure up, you're not good enough or smart enough or appreciated enough. Oh, you may be a big success in some ways, yet whatever you do, it's not enough to fill that empty, dead feeling inside, it's not enough to chase away the blackness concealed in your heart.

You probably haven't told anyone about that black rotten spot eating away at the center of your being. It's filled with envy and fear, bitterness and desire. Your most secret feelings and thoughts are stored there, ugly things, so dark, so cold, so mean, it seems impossible that other people can't look right into your eyes and see the badness lurking inside you, skulking in the corners of the rag-and-bone shop of your heart.

"I celebrate and sing myself," Walt Whitman wrote with exuberance. "Clear and sweet is my soul . . ." But if you were to sing your own soul, it would be a dull and dolorous dirge. It would be a bitter aimless noise, more akin to a wail than a melody.

You may feel like the person in Stephen Crane's poem:

I stood upon a high place,
And saw, below, many devils
Running, leaping,
And carousing in sin.
One looked up, grinning,
And said, "Comrade! Brother!"

A cold hell, a solitary confinement — that's what your self feels like at zero level. I know you don't want to talk about the secret darkness that makes you hate yourself. Such words bring a stiffening of the body, a turning away of the countenance. Sometimes the terrible reality is accepted . . . with tears.

You think you are alone.

You are wrong.

You think the only way to deal with the darkness in your heart is to hide it.

You are wrong again.

You are suffering, in part, because in P.S. Dread you learned to judge yourself and others with a distorted set of values. Your experiences in your alcoholic family taught you to believe that normal feelings are bad. This meant that in order to be "good" you had to be perfect, so this warped logic led you to believe that perfection was normal.

Since the ideal of perfection is impossible to attain — let alone to maintain — self-hate and misery followed.

"Lord," prayed Sir Thomas Browne, "Lord, deliver me from myself."

Alcoholic families kill self-esteem. This is a reality. Once we truly accept that our self-hate is a direct result of the rules and values and behaviors we learned in our alcoholic families, we can transcend our sense of worthlessness. Because once we truly accept this reality, we can change it. We can create a new reality, write a new equation of self.

We can make up new rules.

We can discover new values.

We can change our behavior.

We can accept ourselves.

We can finally be free from the torment of self-hate.

15

Confronting
Your Inner Parent

To reach the clearing beyond, we must stay with the weightless journey through uncertainty. Whatever counterfeit safety we hold from overinvestments in people and institutions must be given up. The inner custodian must be unseated from the controls. No foreign power can direct our journey from now on. It is for each of us to find a course that is valid by our own reckoning

— Gail Sheehy, Passages

Not long ago I watched a group of children playing games down the street. A small boy, about four years old with blond hair and an impish grin, seemed to be making up his own rules. Whenever he got the chance, he'd grab the ball and run with it tucked tightly into his belly, his head bent low as he charged down the street like a miniature defensive lineman screaming gleefully, "Mine! Mine! Mine!"

One of the other children, a girl about age seven with cornsilk hair matching the boy's, fumed indignantly at this infraction of the rules. She stood with her feet firmly planted on the pavement, fists on her hips, elbows jutting out at the sides, jaw thrust forward. "You stop that right now, Jimmy!" she bellowed. "Do you hear me?"

How could he not hear her? Her voice had the volume and timbre of a diminutive drill sergeant. But it didn't have much effect on Jimmy. He turned around, made a face at his sister, then ran away.

"You're in trouble now, young man," the little girl hollered, sounding for all the world like a distraught mother ready to snap. "You get back here right now! Do you hear me? You're gonna give me a nervous breakdown! Can't you act right?"

The front door of a nearby house flew open and a woman appeared, hands on hips, feet wide apart, chin thrust forward. "You kids get in this house right now! Do you hear me? Can't you even play for five minutes without fighting? Get in here! Now!"

The Importance of Acting Right

Earlier we spoke of the frightened inner child each of us carries with us — the part of us that is vulnerable and insecure and needy. The inner child is one aspect of self, one of the pieces in the complex puzzle that is our identity.

Each of us also possesses another aspect of self — the inner parent.

The inner parent is akin to conscience. It is the internalized messages, values, rules and feelings that control our behavior and keeps us from behaving like savages.

It's also the beliefs and feelings and self-justifications that at times make us behave like punitive jerks, insufferable asses and self-righteous prigs.

And it is the inner parent that makes us want to control the behavior of other people. We want them to act right, shape up, use their heads, have a little will power and for God's sake, start treating us the way they should.

---

*In alcoholic families control is the most fundamental and basic
issue for every family member.*

Why do control issues take on such an overwhelming
importance? Because the family is out of control. Totally and
completely. No one will talk about it, of course, unless they
are complaining, blaming or making excuses. Yet every
member of the family senses the tension, feels the apprehen-
sion and worries late at night about how to fix the whole
mess up. How, we wonder, can we make these people act
right? What is it we need to do to make everything better?

This preoccupation with the need to control ourselves and
the people around us is such an integral part of the alcoholic
family that I have not yet met an adult child who wasn't
bursting at the seams with the need to make people
(including themselves) act right.

But what is Acting Right?

If our own needs and wants and desires are unfulfilled, if
we are self-absorbed, hungry for recognition and admiration, then acting right is easily defined. Other people are
acting right when they—

— share our beliefs and biases.
— recognize our innate superiority.
— let us have our own way.
— depend on our knowledge and wisdom.
— hold us up in awe and admiration.
— approve us, love us and don't criticize us.

We, in turn, are acting right whenever we behave in a
manner that makes other people act right.

To a certain degree the desire to influence our family and
friends to share our beliefs or to behave decently or to hold
us in high esteem is normal. But in alcoholic families this
normal tendency is carried to destructive extremes.

Whether we recognize it or not, making parents, lovers,
children, siblings, friends, neighbors, co-workers, grocery
store clerks, strangers and small household appliances act
right becomes the major focus of our lives.

Even after intensive therapy, the need to control is so deeply ingrained in adult children I don't think we can ever be completely cured of it. One of the most amusing sights around is a room full of recovering, self-actualizing, professional care-giving adult children of alcoholics jockeying for recognition and power and control. And all the while keeping the determined pasted-on smiles grimly in place and trying valiantly not to let therapeutic levels of unconditional positive regard slip away because to show publicly that you considered all these other guys misguided fools and that you wanted to be powerful and controlling and the center of attention wouldn't be acting right!

The point is this: For adult children, over-sized egos, an excessive need to be in control and an excessive preoccupation with wishing to be recognized and admired is and always will be a major aspect of our character.

We can deal with this unflattering truth in several ways:

- We can deny it and continue conducting our lives as usual.
- We can brood about it, beating ourselves over the head for a while and hope it will go away.
- Or we can accept it with good humor and learn to live with it.

And when we marvel at all the self-centered egotists we encounter in our everyday lives, we might reflect on our own egotistical needs, recalling Ambrose Bierce's definition of an egotist:

"A person of low taste, more interested in himself than in me."

Power, Control and Manipulation

In alcoholic families the underlying issue in every argument is a bitter conflict over who is right, who is in authority, who has the power and who is in control. Whether our inner parent is a healthy guide to moral conduct or a punitive and manipulative spirit depends in large part on the teachings we received from our real parents as we watched or participated in family conflict.

Figuring out who's trying to control what in an alcoholic family can be both frustrating and confusing. While one family member may appear dominant (loud, angry, aggressive) and another submissive (fearful, passive, depressed), it is important to note that the undercurrent of family dynamics can be quite different than surface appearances.

The alcoholic male who rages when his intimidated wife dares to use the telephone, who controls the bank accounts and who makes jealous accusations when his wife is 15 minutes late coming home from the grocery store, may seem like the master of the household, yet in reality he may feel totally dependent on and at the mercy of his wife and children. His violent outbursts and stony silences are his way of defending against feelings of weakness, helplessness or impotence. In his own mind he is a besieged man, a victim of unfair circumstances, and his dominating and violent actions are to him justifiable means of regaining his sense of power and control. If he has to hurt others to achieve this . . . well, he's only giving them what they deserve.

Women in alcoholic homes also think of themselves as victims and like men they may adopt manipulative strategies aimed at giving themselves power and control in the family. The seemingly passive mother who appears to be a doormat may in reality be in tight control of her family.

A woman who is dependent on the achievements and support of her husband or children for her own sense of self-esteem may use exaggerated displays of hurt feelings and martyrdom to force the support and submissiveness of others. Her two main weapons are physical illness and emotional liability. When the going gets rough, she gets sick . . . or hysterical . . . or depressed.

She seldom asks for help directly. In fact, she usually tells her family, "Don't worry about me. You're more important." She takes the martyr's stance, generating guilt in others and using her self-punitive behavior as a way to induce her family to protect and take care of her. Because she is sick or nervous or sad, she is excused from being a fully functioning self-fulfilling person. Full of guilt and resentment, her family grudgingly adjusts to her needs. She's in control. She wins . . . or so she thinks.

These are but two of many control strategies children learn in alcoholic families. These strategies are obviously dysfunctional, and they increase pain and resentment and alienation. But they work.

As an adult child named Edna told me, "My mother always makes a big production about how she doesn't want to be an interfering mother and about how free I am to do whatever I want to do with my life. But whenever I do something she doesn't like — if I apply for a job in another city or if I say I'm not coming for Sunday dinner, within 24 hours she has one of her terrible asthma attacks. She can't breathe. She calls me up gasping, and I have to come running over and rush her to the hospital. She really is sick. The doctor says that when she gets like that she could die if she doesn't get quick treatment."

What's the message Edna's getting? Do something that makes your mother unhappy and she'll die. "So what do I do?" asks Edna with bitter resignation in her voice. "You know damn good and well what I do! I come running!"

Edna fairly vibrates with rage when she talks about her mother. "I tell you, that woman can walk through a field of ragweed without a sniffle, but if I say I'm not going to spend Thanksgiving Day with her and the rest of the family, she's on oxygen and life support by sunset."

Edna came into therapy feeling depressed and totally overwhelmed by daily life. She felt like a victim . . . of her mother, her husband, her boss, her in-laws. She believed she was being constantly manipulated by their unfair efforts to control every aspect of her life. She felt powerless.

During our conversations, Edna's language was peppered with phrases like —

— my mother should . . .
— if only my husband would . . .
— my father-in-law ought to . . .
— they should know that . . .

Underneath her outward pleasantness and concern for the well-being of the people she loved, Edna was unrelentingly critical and disapproving toward all the people who were close to her. Her comments were frequently two-edged. "I'm so lucky to be married to a man as wonderful as Zack . . . if only he was more competent at his job and made more money." "Zack is such a sweet, old-fashioned romantic but . . . he has such terrible timing."

Over time questions began to form: Was Edna's problem that she was being controlled? Or was she miserable because of her excessive need to be controlling? Was it possible that Edna was caught in one of the paradoxes of self-esteem?

Is it possible that we feel the most manipulated and controlled when we fail in our attempts to control and manage the behavior of others?

After several months Edna answered the question herself. "You know," she said, "I'm always in a dither because the people I care about don't do things the way I think they should. Take my mother, for example. I've always felt she was pulling my strings, but I'm beginning to see that I pull her strings, too. I'm always trying to make her act different. I'm always full of helpful hints. Lose weight. Dye your hair. Go to night school. Don't let Dad walk on you. Speak up. Be more assertive. Get in touch with your feelings. Get out more." Edna paused and thought for a moment. "All those suggestions are really veiled criticism. Good Lord, I've been judgmental toward her! And it seems like her asthma attacks come on after I've given her a good lecture on how to improve herself. It's like we're locked in this mortal battle to see who can exert the most influence over the other. I nag and defy. She gets sick. I think maybe I'm going to work on being less negative with her and see what happens."

That was two difficult years ago. Edna has totally eliminated the words "My mother should . . ." from her vocabulary. Mother still has asthma attacks. The last one was six months ago. And she'll probably have more in the future. But not every week like she used to have.

Edna's frustration quotient has gone down considerably. But she hasn't reached Nirvana yet. Edna is still working on: "Zack's a wonderful husband, but . . ."

Being Controlled
By Your Inner Parent

Too often children raised in alcoholic families develop an inner parent that is stern, intimidating, disapproving, critical and self-righteous. Edna discovered this to be true in her case. When she worked on changing the voice of her inner parent to a more positive and accepting chord, she changed her life.

The voice of our inner parent develops early.

Even as adults we can all recognize aspects of this early imitative process in ourselves. Susan, for example, cocks her head and rolls her eyes just like her mother. Steve contemplatively strokes his beardless chin, much the same way his bearded father did when lost in thought. But the mimicking of Mom and Dad go far beyond stroking the chin and rolling the eyes.

At age seven the little blond girl playing in the street already displayed an amazing repertoire of controlling, intimidating and critical behaviors. Without conscious effort, she had adopted and accepted her harried mother's behavior as normal and right and worthy. She had internalized the messages her mother had given her and made them part of her own identity.

And whether we like it or not, the voice of our own inner parent will remain an unpleasant echo from the terrible past unless we begin to work through the distorted and negative internalized messages we received from our real parents when they were sick, confused, hurting and least able to provide us with positive lessons.

If our inner parent is stern, critical and disapproving, it will not permit us to love and enjoy our real parents, our spouses or our children. It will force us to feel judgmental and victimized at every turn. No matter how noble our motives or how sincere our efforts to love and care for the people close to us, our disapproving inner parent will sooner or later get in the way of harmony.

A client of mine named Kevin is both a son of an alcoholic and an alcoholic himself. He readily admits that during his drinking days he was insensitive, preoccupied with himself, surly toward his wife and children and unreasonably demanding.

"I always had to be right," he admits. "I put Ilene down a lot, blamed her for my problems. I never listened to her or the boys. All of our conversations were one-way monologues with me interrupting, bragging, moralizing, preaching, blaming or giving orders. I thought if she would only do what I thought she should, if she'd act the way a wife was supposed to, then we wouldn't have so many problems."

By the time Kevin was 30, his drinking was out of control. Desperate, Ilene threatened him with divorce.

"Go ahead and get your damn divorce," Kevin responded defiantly. "I don't care."

Less than a week later Kevin was picked up for drunk driving. When his boss heard about it, Kevin lost his job (which entailed driving clients in a company car). The judge gave Kevin a choice: Alcoholism treatment or jail.

Kevin checked into an in-patient program.

And Ilene filed for divorce.

In treatment Kevin underwent a transformation. With sobriety came a spiritual awakening and a new understanding of the pain he had caused Ilene and his sons with his drinking and surly behavior. He turned his life over to his Higher Power and immersed himself in Alcoholics Anonymous.

And he realized how much he loved Ilene and the boys. Family took on a new importance. "I don't want the divorce," Kevin told me. "I need to show Ilene that I've changed. I'm not the same person I was before."

How did he go about trying to change Ilene's mind? Why, by showing her how spiritual he was now and by letting her know that if she would only get as spiritual as he was, their troubles would be over.

"I'm really worried about the boys," he confided. "If the divorce goes through, I'm going to have to sue for custody. Ilene isn't doing anything about their spiritual education. And, you know, her brother smokes marijuana. That's not a good influence on them. Ilene says she doesn't let him do it around them, but I don't think she's providing them with the proper moral environment. We need to be together again as a family, but she still says she wants a divorce. She says she doesn't trust me, that I killed our marriage and she's right. But I'm changed. She's got to see that I'm not the same man I was before."

Several weeks later all hell broke loose. Kevin discovered that Ilene had renewed a sexual affair with an old boyfriend. "She lied to me," he said, aghast. "All this time, she's insisted that starting a new relationship was the farthest thing from her mind. Now I find out she's been lying to me the whole time."

Kevin confronted her with the facts. He told her he still loved her and wanted to save their marriage despite the fact that she was a liar and an immoral person. Now that he was so spiritual he could call upon his Higher Power to give him the strength to forgive her for messing up so badly. But if she still insisted on the divorce, he was going to drag her and her boyfriend and their "sex orgies" through the mud, and he was going to get custody of the kids. She could go off whoring all she wanted, but by God, not around his sons, she couldn't. They needed a moral home and he was going to make sure they got it.

"I don't know what's wrong," Kevin wailed. "I love her. I want to save our marriage. I'm willing to forgive her for all she's done. Why can't she see how much I've changed from the drinking days?"

Maybe because he hadn't changed enough.

Before treatment, Kevin had been a drinking, insensitive, prideful, punitive, boastful, intimidating, self-righteous man who wanted to solve his problems by making his wife act right.

After treatment, he was a non-drinking, insensitive, prideful, punitive, boastful, intimidating, self-righteous man who wanted to solve his problems by making his wife act right.

Big change!

With less than two month's sobriety under his belt, Kevin was now judge and jury on how to conduct a moral life. He was an instant expert. While drinking he had lied constantly, picked up women in bars for one-night stands, neglected his children, squandered money and jeopardized his family's future. Yet with hardly a twinge of conscience, he condemned Ilene as a liar, a sinner and a whore for behavior that was no worse than his own.

Kevin even started applying for jobs as an alcohol counselor. "I want to help people," he told me. "I have a lot to offer."

He certainly did — self-righteous opinions, accusations, moralistic platitudes, cracker barrel philosophy, disapproval and an inner parent with a harshly judgmental, punitive voice.

Kevin's recovery is complicated by the fact that on the surface he is one of the wittiest and most charming fellows you would ever want to meet. He smiles easily. His laugh is infectious. He's a wonderful salesman and it's hard not to like him.

Like many adult children, Kevin covers up his real feelings with a congenial mask. But deep inside, he has an image of himself and the world as he thinks it ought to be, which is in continual conflict with how it really is.

He is in constant conflict with the people he loves because on both a conscious and unconscious level he is driven to restructure his world to conform to the impossible standards of his demanding and disapproving inner parent.

In many ways Kevin and many other adult children are similar to the little seven-year-old girl standing in the street screaming after her brother, "Can't you act right?"

By the time we reach adulthood that voice has buried itself deep into our unconscious, yet it still calls out, the voice of our inner parent demanding in a tone only we can hear: Act Right!

The voice of the adult child's inner parent is typically controlling, disapproving, harsh and judgmental, and it gets in the way of loving relationships with our real parents, our spouses, siblings, children and friends.

For many of us the problems caused by our preoccupation with control are not as obvious as Kevin's. Still, our lives are filled with conflicts caused by our unconscious need to have our own way.

Because Kevin sincerely wants to recover, he is in the process of confronting his demanding inner parent. He's learning techniques that allow him more emotional freedom. He's also become aware that letting go of control — learning to live and let live — is risky.

When we relinquish control, we must adopt new attitudes that say:

- I believe other people have the capacity to function in a competent fashion.
- I will allow other people to be responsible for their own behavior.
- I will experience moments of anxiety, awkwardness or uncertainty, and I can do this without falling apart.
- I will allow other people to take credit for their own successes and failures.
- I admit that opinions, beliefs or customs different from my own may be of equal or superior value.
- I admit my own fallibility.
- I set aside the importance of always winning.
- I will show respect and support for the ideas and actions of people who may differ from myself.
- I will abandon my self-righteous desire to be superior to others.

Letting go of control fosters independence in the people we love, and that can be scary. Will they become so independent that they will no longer want or need us? Will they abandon us? Reject us? Hate us?

Perhaps.

It seems far more likely that we will drive the people we love away from us with our insufferably self-righteous, disapproving and critical attempts to make them act right.

Our judgmental, disapproving inner parent prevents us from truly communicating with the people we love because instead of really listening with an ear toward understanding and sharing, we are busy mentally preparing our rebuttal. Like Kevin, we preach, moralize, criticize, distance, degrade, devalue, brag and dispense advice. Usually unsolicited advice.

None of these activities has anything to do with listening. Yet more than anything else, I think all of us want to be listened to and understood.

We can never underestimate the psychological healing power of the simple act of listening.

When we listen to another person without expressing criticism or disapproval, when we let them talk without forcing our own opinion on them, we are allowing understanding and positive self-esteem to grow. We are demonstrating that —

- we care.
- we value that person even when we disagree with them.
- we have faith in their ability to competently deal with their own life.
- we respect that person's intelligence.
- we are letting that person know they are not alone in an uncaring world.

Empathetic Listening

Empathy is an understanding so intimate that the feelings, thoughts and motives of one person are readily comprehended by another.

We sometimes try to show empathy by saying, "I know how you feel," or "Exactly the same thing happened to me." If we then follow up with a description of our feelings, thoughts, problems or trials and tribulations, we are not showing empathy at all. We are like thoughtless children vying for recognition: "Me first! Me first! Listen to me!" We hog the conversation, and we put a barrier (our own ego) in the way of true communication.

Self absorption and empathy are incompatible traits. How can we possibly comprehend the feelings, thoughts and motives of another person when we're all wrapped up in our own concerns? Empathetic listening means putting your own concerns and judgments aside for a few minutes and listening to your spouse or parent or child or friend so that you understand the feelings underneath the spoken words.

Sounds easy, doesn't it?

It isn't. In alcoholic families, family members talk at each other, not with each other. The majority of dialogues are really double monologues. Dad spouts off his demands and rationalizations. Mom waits for him to pause for breath and when he does, she launches into her own agenda, her own demands and rationalizations. They are like debate opponents vying for advantage, seeking to score points. The purpose of these conversations is to influence, persuade, browbeat, manipulate, guilt-trip and generally convince the opposition to act right.

Not surprisingly, most adult children adopt the communication style they learned from Mom and Dad.

Quite often I hear adult children complain that their parents never listened to them. These feelings spill over into other relationships — with lovers, co-workers, our children. We feel alone and misunderstood.

Yet how many of us realize that our parents, lovers, friends and children have just as great a need for us to understand and listen to them. If we want to be understood, perhaps we first need to stop judging, disapproving and criticizing those around us. Empathetic listening is a skill we can learn to help us make emotional connections with the people we love.

Here are some rules for empathetic listening:

• *Don't assume that the person you are listening to expects you to come up with a solution to his or her problems.*

Many times all we really want is a sounding board. For example, a friend of mine named Ralph was encountering some serious problems with his 23-year-old daughter Jenna. They'd always had a close relationship, but lately they seemed to argue constantly. Jenna admitted that she was feeling resentful towards him. "He's gotten so bossy and interfering and critical lately. He's driving me nuts."

What was happening was this: Jenna had taken a demanding new job which was consuming most of her waking thoughts. When she visited her father, conversation usually centered on her job, its complexities, challenges and difficulties. She'd vent about problems with co-workers, confusion over policies, struggles for recognition.

Ralph, with his many years of business experience, wanted to help his daughter succeed. He'd listen for a moment, analyze the situation and plot a strategy for her. He'd say, "What you need to do, honey, is . . ."

Whenever Ralph used those words, Jenna wanted to scream, "If I want your advice, I'll ask for it!"

And that was the crux of the problem. Ralph felt he was supposed to solve his "little girl's" problems, tell her what to do, make everything better for her.

All Jenna wanted was a sounding board for her excitement, triumphs, frustrations and fear. When Ralph realized Jenna neither expected nor wanted him to come up with solutions, a tremendous burden was lifted and the closeness returned to their relationship.

• *Don't minimize their concerns or worries by telling them about somebody else who has real problems, changing the subject or telling them they are making a big deal out of nothing.*

Once when I was teaching a seminar, a shy teenage girl came to see me after class about an intimate and embarrassing physical problem. She had an undeveloped third nipple on her chest. While this minor defect posed no risk to her health, it was the sort of thing that would cause anguish to any normally sensitive girl. Because correcting her problem would require a relatively inexpensive medical procedure, I suggested she discuss the intensity of her feelings with her parents. She returned several days later to report that she had sincerely tried to express her embarrassment and despondency to her parents, but they had "pooh-poohed" her concerns, telling her she was making a mountain out of a molehill — and chuckling at the pun. "You should be grateful you don't have any real problems," they told her.

They refused to discuss the situation further. It was only after their daughter attempted to perform surgery on herself in the family bathroom that her parents reacted. "Why didn't you tell us it bothered you so much," they asked. "I did," she responded. "But you didn't listen."

• *Don't act superior by saying, "Well, what I would do is . . ."*

When we start explaining what we'd do, we have stopped listening and started talking, making ourselves the center of attention while at the same time implying we can quickly and easily come up with a plan of action that the other poor boob is too dumb or weak to figure out for himself. It's remarkably easy to say . . .

"Well, I wouldn't take that kind of crap."

"I'd divorce the dirty S.O.B."

"I'd knock my kid silly if he talked to me like that."

"I wouldn't care if he is the boss. I wouldn't let anyone push me around."

Why is it that we can be confident, assertive, wise and righteous when solving another person's problems? But when it comes to solving our own problems, well . . .

• *Don't feel that you have to agree 100% with everything they say in order to be empathetic.*

A person who came of age in the 1960s or 1970s is likely to have a world view quite different from someone who lived through the Great Depression and World War II. Values change. Goals change. Styles change.

Changes inevitably create a fertile breeding ground for conflict, especially for adults who have conflicts with both their own parents and their own children. This isn't a generation gap, it's a generation squeeze from both directions, and when we're squeezed too hard, we reflexively push back against the pressure with all our might.

Undeniably, alcoholic and co-dependent parents possess many personality and character traits which make them difficult to deal with in a loving manner. But what good is it to blame and resent them for attitudes and behaviors they've had for a lifetime? We can improve our relationships if we become more accepting and less blaming.

Now, you may be asking: Why bother?

Unless you make the effort to learn how to communicate more effectively and lovingly with your parents, there is a very real danger that you will perpetuate with your own children the same kinds of conflicts and barriers to loving that you have with your parents.

When you were born, your parents were supposed to suddenly become child-care experts. They weren't ready. They had not solved their own problems yet.

Are you ready? Have you solved your problems yet? A loving parent will not force the same pattern of conflict on their son and daughter. If you can learn to accept and value your turbulent parents, you are setting a good example for your own children to follow.

Your parents may be critical of the way you live your life and the way you raise your children. It's natural for you to want to make your parents see the validity of your lifestyle and values. It is just as natural for them to try to make you live according to their rules. This conflict between parent and child is as old as humankind itself, and it will probably continue forever.

So it is pointless to resent your parents or argue with them or try to change them when they express a deeply felt opinion that differs from your own.

They have a right to their beliefs.

And so do you.

The bottom line is this: You don't have to live your life according to their rules. And they don't have to live according to yours.

You don't have to live your life according to their rules. And they don't have to live according to yours.

By listening to your parents when they criticize you, rather than attacking them or blaming them, you may generate a more caring less hostile atmosphere.

This doesn't mean you have to agree with them. Listening to their point of view and acknowledging their right to their own opinion simply gives them an important sense of being taken into account, which we all need. Empathetic listening can drastically cut down on the need to endlessly defend your own position and point of view from attack.

For example, your mother says indignantly, "I don't think a couple should live together without marriage. A man won't buy a cow when the milk is free."

Instead of shouting, "I'm not a cow and this isn't a dairy I'm running here, so mind your own damn business!". . .

. . .You might make eye contact with your mother, nod your head slightly, and say, "I can see how you feel that way."

What does it hurt to let her have her say? What does it hurt to listen to her, to nod your head and say, "I understand what you're saying to me. Thank you for being concerned."

If in August your mother calls you long distance and says, "I don't know what I'll do if the whole family doesn't get together this Christmas," what does it hurt to respond, "I know how important family traditions are to you, Mom, and next November when we start making plans for Christmas, I'll let you know right away if we're going to be able to visit you."

If your father-in-law sees your child snuggled up in bed with the cat and intones, "We never allowed animals in the house," what does it hurt to say, "I know you feel strongly about that."

Sometimes, simply making eye contact and saying, "I understand," is enough. You are acknowledging they have a valid point of view. It just happens to be different from your own, equally valid, point of view.

Caring people can disagree on many issues and still care about each other.

If your parents feel you are taking their opinions into account, if they don't feel the sting of your rejection, they may surprise you by backing off a little. Think about this for a moment. Your own observations will tell you that we feel the most need to repeatedly hammer home our own point of view when the person we are talking to refuses to listen to us. The more someone fights us, the more effort we put into trying to convince them of the rightness of our position. And oddly enough we are less likely to try to impose our will on people who listen to us openly . . . even when we continue to disagree with each other.

By listening to their point of view with empathy, you are not giving into their demands. You are listening. You are opening the door for a calmer discussion. You might learn something from them, for it is rare to find any individual who is 100% wrong about everything. You may, for the first time in your life, have a chance to express your own views to them in a rational, adult manner. Maybe you won't change their minds. Maybe you will. Maybe it doesn't really matter whether you convince each other.

Remember as long as you are an adult, supporting yourself and not asking your parents to take care of you, you don't have to live by their rules. And they don't have to live by yours.

You don't have to be in control.

Why can't people who love each other accept each other? The problem is the past. We interpret today through yesterday. Nobody is listening in the present. We are listening instead to all the pain and hurt and conflict from the past. We all cling to yesterday. And because we cling to yesterday, we become unavailable to today.

We spend our whole lives pushing against the past, fighting unnecessary battles of pride.

If your parent or spouse or child is stubborn, infuriating, opinionated, controlling and pushy, what will it hurt if you stop pushing back?

Try to understand. When you push against a strong opposing force, you both remain stuck in one spot. You hold each other rigid. Move aside. Stop pushing. Without your resistance to hold it up, the opposition may collapse.

Take a chance.

Stop pushing.

16

Transformations

Living well is the best revenge.

— *George Herbert*

In the beginning we said this book was about confronting and changing ourselves, not about confronting and changing our parents. Many of us yearn for the power to rewrite the script of our lives, starting out by changing the character of our parents. It's always tempting to begin our own self-renewal and transformation by reforming the behavior of someone else.

Too many of us have been almost obsessed with the idea of transforming our parents and our families. In our fantasies we straighten things out, fix things up, create love and warmth and harmony. We share the truth with them, we enlighten them, and the scales will drop from their eyes. Everyone lives happily ever after.

Then there are darker fantasies, the ones where we get even, when we have it out with the mother or father who hurt us. To a certain degree, this fantasy is a power trip. We are strong. Invincible. We hurl the truth in the face of our cringing parents. We make them pay for their crimes against us. We say all the words we saved up over a lifetime of hurt.

"Don't you know how that made me feel?" we yell in their face. And we make them know. We make them feel our pain.

If your parents are still mired down in alcoholism or co-dependency, you may feel that you will never be able to find happiness unless your parents change.

Your recovery does not depend upon the recovery of your parents.

It is helpful if the alcoholic quits drinking, but we can begin our own recovery even if their alcoholism and co-dependency continue. Your recovery is not measured by changes in the behavior of your parents. It is measured by your own growth and power to control your own life.

If you understand all of this and you still want to do something about your parent's drinking. You have a couple of workable options . . .

1. You can detach yourself emotionally from your mother's or father's disease without totally removing them from your life. This means that you learn how to stop taking responsibility for your parent's illness and start taking responsibility for yourself. This is an approach advocated by Al-Anon.

Al-Anon is made up of women and men who love an alcoholic and who are struggling to find peace and happiness. It can help you deal with your guilt and fear and your need to control. Al-Anon is listed in the phone book. There are also a number of Adult Children of Alcoholics (ACoA or ACA) groups springing up around the country. There might be one in your community. Check it out.

2. You can instigate a professional, structured intervention aimed at getting your alcoholic parent into treatment. We used to believe that you couldn't force a person to seek help until they wanted it. We now know that we no longer have to wait for the alcoholic to want help. We can make them want help. This is done through a process called intervention.

Almost all professional chemical dependency treatment units have intervention teams who specialize in creating a well-thought-out, dispassionate, lovingly firm confrontation between the alcoholic and the people who care about him or her. During the confrontation, family and friends tell the alcoholic how the drinking or drug use is causing problems, that treatment is necessary and that they are committed to participating in treatment as a family.

Intervention can be a highly effective means of getting chemically dependent people into treatment. Celebrities such as Betty Ford and Elizabeth Taylor credit family intervention with saving their lives.

A cautionary note: Intervention is a rehearsed, structured confrontation . . . not a typical family fight. Trying it on your own will probably be no more effective than any other family brawl. Most major chemical dependency programs will offer consultation on the intervention process free of charge or at low cost. If you really want to do something about your mother's or father's drinking, professional intervention is an option worth trying.

When Nothing Works

What options do you have if your mother or father is physically, sexually or emotionally abusive? What do you do if the abuse that hurt you as a child, now endangers your own children? What do you do if after your best efforts, the relationship between you and your parent remains impossible, destructive or dangerous?

In some cases it is helpful, even necessary, for us to physically distance ourselves from our parents. Sometimes we must terminate all contact with one or both of our parents in order to survive. Time and distance may — repeat, may — lessen the pain and heal the wounds. If not, then we may have to wish our parent well and in our minds kiss him or her good-bye.

Having It Out

Many adult children feel that their recovery will be facilitated by "having it out" with their mom or dad. This usually means they want to confront their mother or father with a list of grievances detailing the hurts inflicted on the innocent child through the carelessness, indifference, neglect or meanness of the abusive parent.

Some therapists recommend this as a good way to clear the air. I caution against this unless . . .

1. The confrontation takes place as part of a structured process facilitated by a professional therapist.

2. It is handled in a loving and non-judgmental fashion with the aim of increasing family communication and intimacy.

3. The interaction is a two-way exchange in which the parent is also allowed to express both positive and negative feelings.

Wait just a minute. Stop right here, I can hear you saying, "But my mother would never agree to family counseling. If I do what you say, I'll never get a chance to tell her about all the terrible ways she hurt me. I'll never get these feelings off my chest."

Well . . . maybe you'll never be able to spew venom and hate and vituperation in the face of your mother and father.

But stop for a moment of total honesty. Think about it . . . In your secret heart of hearts, in your darkest moments of fantasy isn't that what you want . . . to punish your parents, to lay blame, to retaliate for the hurt they have caused you?

Too often "clearing the air" is an excuse for claiming revenge, for blame-gaming. And therapy can degenerate into parent-bashing sessions, whether the parents are actually present or not.

Is that what you really want?

If you have the urge to "have it out" with one of your parents I ask you to wait . . . reconsider. Go back to the first five chapters of this book. Practice the Forgiveness Exercises in chapters Four and Five.

Suffering lives on resentment — the more resentment, the more nourishment there is for suffering. If you want to keep suffering, you cannot forgive, you cannot let go of the past, particularly the hurts, the humiliations, the wounds, the insults, the living nightmares of your childhood pain.

If you master the art of forgiveness, if you practice the Forgiveness Exercises as they are outlined, if you become willing to let go of the past, if you confront your inner parent and inner child . . .

. . . you will no longer need to punish and harangue your real parent with a list of grievances and pain. You will no longer need to carry the torch of family pain from one generation to the next.

Shared Guilt

One Sunday night Annie was on the verge of having it out with her mother. Although Annie now had a child of her own, she was still obsessed with thoughts of how her mother had betrayed her, intimidated her, made her feel unwanted and unloved as both a child and an adult. Annie hated the way she still felt dependent and controlled by her mother's moods and demands.

Annie sat in her mother's armchair knitting and fuming, as she did every Sunday night. It was a regular routine. On Sunday night, Dad went to his A.A. meeting and Annie and her son, Eric, visited Mom. Eric played with toy soldiers on the carpet while Mama and Grandma knitted and talked.

On this Sunday, Annie's mother must have felt the tension in the air. She looked at her grandson on the floor and said, "I love you, Eric."

He replied mechanically without raising his head. "Love you, too, Grandma."

The older woman glanced at her daughter and sighed. "You're lucky you didn't know your grandmother, Annie. She was a real witch. I hated her."

Annie looked up startled. "You hated your own mother?"

"She hated me."

Annie was shocked. "Oh, Mother," Annie said. "Your own mother couldn't have hated you."

Mom shook her head. "You think that because you always knew you were loved. I vowed I'd never do to you what my mother did to me. I'd never say or do anything to make you feel unloved or unwanted." The older woman looked straight in her daughter's eyes. "I always did my best to let you know how important you are to me."

Annie sat frozen in her chair, staring at her mother. She felt like she was losing her mind. Didn't her mother know how it had made young Annie feel to hear her mother shout . . .

"Will you please leave me alone for five minutes."

"Go outside and play."

"Can't you see that I'm busy."

"No, Mommy will not play with you. Mommy has grown-up work to do. Now go to your room and be quiet."

There were thousands of other incidents, insults, rebuffs and rejections. Didn't her mother realize how that had made her feel?

Just then, Eric pulled at her leg. "Hey, Mom —"

"Shhhh, son, Mommy's busy."

She pulled up short. Her response had been automatic, reflexive and it was matched by a thousand other incidents, insults, rebuffs and rejections. None of them meant to hurt.

She looked down at her young son, knowing he was the heart and the light of her life, knowing how much she loved him, knowing that she had vowed to never say or do the things her mother had done to her . . .

. . . and now realizing that she was doing to her son what her mother had done to her, and her grandmother to her mother.

Where did it stop? Where did the cycle of blame and silent recrimination end?

Annie pulled Eric up into a loving embrace. "I love you, son," she said. And looking over his silky hair, she smiled across at her mother, tears in her eyes. "And I love you, Mom."

"Oh, Annie," her mother said, dropping her knitting. She crossed the room to her daughter and grandson, joining in the warm embrace. "You and Eric mean so much to me."

Seven-year-old Eric wormed his way out of the crush of bodies. Wiping lipstick off his cheek, he said, "Gol! You guys sure are weird tonight."

He didn't know he was watching a major transformation. Annie had realized for the first time that her mother had no more purposely wanted to hurt her than she had ever purposely intended to hurt her own son.

Yet, in all honesty, Annie had to admit that many times she had done and said things that disappointed Eric, made him cry, hurt his feelings. But that didn't mean she didn't love him. And it didn't mean she was a bad mother. It simply meant that she was a fallible human being who sometimes made mistakes. She faced pressures and worries and problems that sometimes made it impossible to meet her son's needs and desires. She had always assumed that he would get over his hurts in time, that he would understand because he would always know how much she loved him.

Just as her own mother had always counted on unexpressed love and time to heal all of Annie's wounds.

She had to ask herself how could she expect Eric to understand, accept and forgive his mother's mistakes if she wasn't willing to forgive her own mother for making the same errors in judgment and behavior?

Where did the blame end and the forgiveness start?

THE ADULT CHILD'S GOLDEN RULE

Live in such a way so that you can expect the same amount of love, acceptance and forgiveness from your children as you showed your parents.

It's up to you whether the Adult Child's Golden Rule becomes a blessing or a curse in your life.

17

Making Your Own Light

Home is where when you have to go there,
They have to take you in.

— *Robert Frost*

Sometimes the bitter memories of youth and estrangement from one's family work themselves out in stunning dreams. Loren Eiseley tells of the unraveling of one such drama in a writer who had been struggling with a novel containing difficult autobiographical episodes.

In a detailed and memorable dream the man found himself on a snowy path leading to his childhood home. It was night. He made his way over the creaking snow to the porch, where he tried to peer through a dark window into his old room.

"Suddenly," the man told Eiseley, "I was drawn into a strange mixture of repulsion and desire to press my face against the glass. I knew intuitively they were all there waiting for me within, if I could but see them. My mother and my father. Those I had loved and those I hated. But the window was black to my gaze."

He hesitated a moment in dreamtime and struck a match. "For an instant in that freezing silence," he reported, "I saw my father's face glimmer wan and remote behind the glass. My mother's face was there with the hard distorted lines that marked her later years."

Emboldened by fury, he overcame his cowardice, cupped the match before his face and stepped forward, "stepped closer, closer toward that dreadful confrontation. As the match guttered down, my face was pressed almost to the glass."

And in that magical warping of time and space that occurs in dreams, he was touched by a transforming truth: "I saw it was my own face into which I stared, just as it was reflected in the black glass. My father's haunted face was but my own. The hard lines upon my mother's aging countenance were slowly reshaping themselves upon my living face . . . It taught me something."

We are never told exactly what it was that he was taught. A story-teller might be tempted to round it off neatly with an ending in which he became reconciled with his family and they lived happily ever after.

But for many of us there is no storybook resolution. There is no pat reconciliation, where we nestle once again warm and secure in the bosom of our family.

As novelist Thomas Wolfe wrote, "You can't go home again." His meaning was clear: You can't return to your childhood, to the parents you have lost and the friends who have drifted away. You can't go home again to dreams of romance, fame and glory, and you can't recapture the "solacements of time and memory".

Wolfe — himself an adult child — found words for adult children everywhere.

When we want to go home, there may be no place to go. Or they won't take us in. And we understand Wolfe's cry, "Come back, lost and by the wind grieved ghosts . . ."

But there is a kind of reconciliation that comes when we look at the scarred knuckles and the textured skin on our hands and see the hand that held us, fed us and pointed out the letters as the story was told. Or when we look in the mirror, rub our eyes and behold the strangely familiar lines of a parent's countenance. It teaches us something.

At such times we may feel a chill, a shock of recognition. But it is a healthy shock, not a shattering one, for in the instant of recognition we have grown resilient, touched with a certain clarity and made whole by the ineluctable sense of continuity in our lives — continuity even in the face of rejection, separation, death.

They faced their lives, we realize, and they did the best they could with the tools they had. And we will face our lives and do the best we can with the tools we have. We can spend our time outside shivering in the snow as we peer in a dark window and whimper like small animals to make the shadowy figures within notice us, love us, make things right.

Or we can make our own light in the darkness.